THE **Dessert Deli**

THE **Dessert Deli**
by Laura Amos

Raspberry
Panna Cotta

Belgian Chocolate
& Salted Caramel
Mini Tarts

Lovingly hand made using only the
finest British sourced ingredients
where possible. Beautifully packaged
with a passion for excellence.

Absolutely Amazing

Ingredients: Fresh cream 57%, milk,
raspberries 12%, sugar, Pork gelatine,
fresh Madagascan vanilla
allergens: contains cow's milk and
may contain traces of nuts.

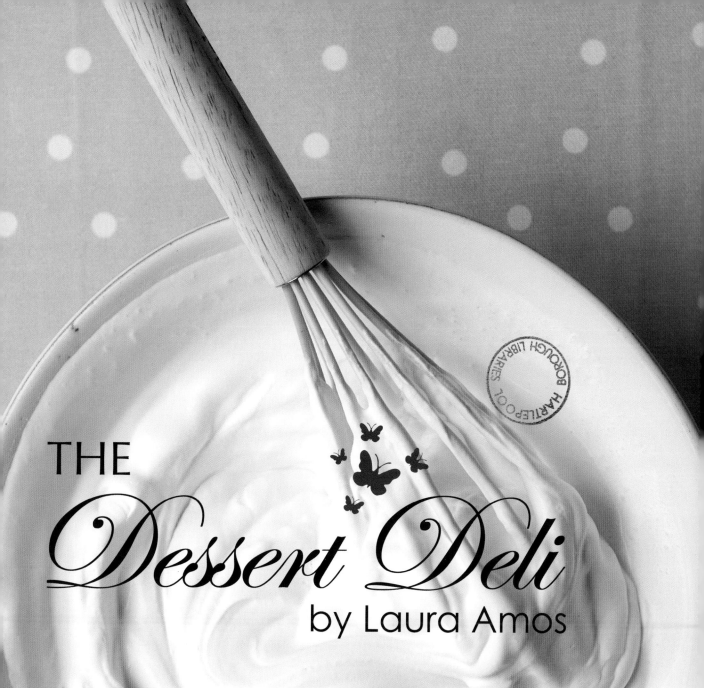

THE

Dessert Deli

by Laura Amos

Paperbooks Publishing, 2 London Wall Buildings,
London EC2M 5UU
info@legend-paperbooks.co.uk
www.legendpress.co.uk

British Library Cataloguing in
Publication Data available.

Print ISBN 978-1-9090390-2-5

Set in Times
Printed by Digital Print Media Ltd

Cover design by Gudrun Jobst www.yotedesign.co.uk
Photography by The Image Pantry
www.theimagepantry.com

PaperBooks

For more information on

The Dessert Deli

visit: www.thedessertdeli.co.uk

or follow Laura on Twitter
@TheDessertDeli

or 'like' The Dessert Deli
on Facebook

This book is dedicated to my amazing Mum.

I thank you from the bottom of my heart, for all your

never-ending support and encouragement. You have been my

inspiration, and I hope I go on to inspire and help others

as you have done to me.

Lots of love

Lou xxx

Contents

GREAT TASTE AWARDS ★ WINNERS

AND ∶BEST∶ ON NORTHCOTE ROAD...

FUDGY, BELGIAN CHOCOLATE BROWNIE...

GOLD 2012 ★

BANOFFEE CHEESECAKE

GOLD 2011 ★

@MasterChef LIVE ∼ PRODUCERS BURSARY AWARD 2010

awarded to producers of excellent British Speciality Foods

Introduction

The Dessert Deli was founded in 2008 on the simple principles of creating affordable yet luxurious handmade desserts using the finest British ingredients where possible. This emphasis on quality soon led the desserts to be stocked in some of the UK's most prestigious food halls including Fortnum & Mason, Selfridges and Harvey Nichols. Today, The Dessert Deli continues to go from strength to strength thanks to a loyal and dedicated customer base as well as a growing range of individual, corporate and retail clients. But even with this burgeoning success, the aforementioned principles have, and always will, remain at the heart of the brand.

Behind the Brand

Laura Amos is the chef/proprietor of The Dessert Deli.

If I'm honest, pastry wasn't my first true passion in the kitchen when I began my life as a chef. However, having to learn the hard way via many mistakes makes you soon wise up and appreciate the precision and skills required to make the perfect dessert.

My first pastry position came as a result of being offered the opportunity to go to London for three months and work under Michelin starred chef Jean-Christophe Novelli, after being fortunate enough to win 'Student of the Year' at college. This initial three month period led to being offered a part-time weekend job, and then a full time position after completing college running the pastry sections at Novelli, W8 and Maison Novelli.

Three years later, I then went on to work at The Ivy. Within a year I had worked my way up through the ranks to Sous Pastry Chef in what proved to be the most challenging, yet inspirational time in my career. I worked at The Ivy for nearly three years and was then offered the role of Head Pastry Chef at Le Caprice, and Caprice Events. Here I worked for two years amongst a great team of chefs, whose passion and dedication for producing top quality food was outstanding. I reluctantly decided to leave to gain more experience and went to work at Popina, an award-winning Artisan bakery. Here I was Head Chef, specialising in product development. This is where I learnt to mass produce products to a high standard using specialist machinery, as well as making handmade products, such as biscotti all cut by hand. This, plus my other experiences, gave me the belief, ability and confidence to follow my dream and start my own unique luxury dessert brand, The Dessert Deli.

The Dessert Deli

In September 2008 at the age of 26, despite being at the height of the recession and my friends thinking I was crazy, I saw a gap in the market for a unique, premium quality dessert brand. Exploding with passion to produce the most luxurious handmade desserts for food lovers, I began my journey.

I started the business baking from my friend's house for my first ever market stall on Balham's Hildreth Street Market in London. As the weeks passed I managed to gain a very loyal network of customers who soon became my friends. So, with business increasingly brisk I quickly outgrew my friend's kitchen – she was delighted – and moved to a shared kitchen in Clapham Junction. A year later I had also outgrown this space and moved into a unit of my own, in which time I'd gained a permanent market pitch on Northcote Road in Clapham Junction. To this day it remains my flagship market stall and where I am still found on a weekly basis, supplying locals with desserts and baked goods and sharing my knowledge of baking. Clapham Junction is now where I call home after leaving Dorset many years ago and the local community I am proud to be a part of.

The online arm of the business and work from retail clients also continues to grow thanks to the success of my range primarily in Selfridges and Fortnum & Mason Food Halls. I've also recently started supplying Whole Foods Market stores, which is hugely exciting as I greatly admire their company ethos. I hope to build a strong working relationship with them, as I have with my other customers. 2012 in particular has proved the most challenging time of my career to date. This summer I have been very privileged and honoured to be involved in some once in a lifetime opportunities, including creating this book.

The Desserts

I believe that consistency is the most important part of any business, and despite our growing workload our desserts are always made to the highest quality, with each and every batch looking and tasting as amazing as the last.

All our products are lovingly made to order, by hand. We use fantastic ingredients from British producers where possible, including British 'Red Tractor' butter, sugar, free range Lion eggs, 'Shipton Mill' flour from Gloucestershire and milk and cream from Hampshire farms. There are a few exceptions which are not British, these include Madagascan vanilla pods and Belgian chocolate but these remain the finest quality ingredients that we can source. All our packaging is carefully selected to make sure it is perfect for every individual item. The product is then labelled by hand and packed, ready for delivery with the utmost care and attention to detail.

Choosing which recipes to include in this book was always going to be a tough task, so who better to ask than The Dessert Deli disciples themselves, my existing customers. They begged, cajoled and demanded to know how to make their favourites (obviously I also made them promise not to stop buying them as well!). My first book is dedicated to my customers whose many favourites I have hopefully included, and to some equally enthusiastic new customers.

The book includes our bestsellers – Belgian Chocolate Mousse with Honeycomb, award-winning Banoffee Cheesecake, and Strawberry Eton Mess – through to the more complex Orange and Passion Fruit Trifle and Prosecco Summer Berry Jelly. I wanted to offer a variety of desserts, some that can be prepared quickly after a hard day at work, through to those more timely creations perfect for showing off at a dinner party.

So please get baking, making and tasting. Enjoy!

Laura Amos

BUTTER

There are several types of butter but sweet cream butter, which is made from pasteurised cream, is the most common type used in the UK. The final product is, by regulation, at least 80% fat, around 16% water and 3% milk solids.

Salted butter is simply butter with the addition of salt to change the flavour.

 CREAM

In the UK the types of cream are legally defined by the percentage of fat that they contain. Creams with a higher fat percentage will be thicker and easier to whip whereas single cream is a lot lower in fat, will not whip and can split easily.

Single cream: contains no less than 18% fat.
Whipping cream: contains no less than 35% fat.
Double cream: contains no less than 48% fat.
Clotted cream: contains no less than 55% fat.

Mascarpone
This is a thick, creamy, soft Italian cheese with a high fat content (40%). An essential ingredient in desserts such as tiramisu.

Cream Cheese
Made from a mixture of cream and milk and eaten fresh. It has a soft, spreadable texture, and a mildly acidic flavour. Most mass-produced versions are pasteurised. In Britain, cream cheese must have a fat content of 45-65% (anything above this is considered double cream cheese). It is great for making cheesecakes.

 EGGS

There has been a big improvement in the quality of eggs and the ethics behind producing them in recent years which has been reflected in the shift to free range eggs by a large percentage of the population. Look for the British Lion mark on the egg shell and egg box - it shows that the eggs have been produced to the highest standards of food safety.

Buy eggs from a reputable retailer where they will have been transported and stored at the correct temperature (below 20°C).

Keep eggs refrigerated and store in their box and, as they are porous, away from strong-smelling foods.

Pasteurised Eggs
These are eggs that have been pasteurised in order to reduce the possibility of food-borne illness in dishes that are not cooked or lightly cooked. They may be sold as liquid egg products or pasteurised in the shell.

 FLOUR

White Flour
Historically, white flour used to be made by sifting the wholemeal flour through linen or silk sifting cloths to separate the coarse bran and the germ from the creamy white starch hidden within the wheat grain. It was always the preserve of the wealthy. Today, everybody can enjoy white flour and it has become the norm.

Plain Flour
Plain flour is a lower protein flour blended so it is 'all purpose' for all household baking needs. Usually used for cakes and pastries and for thickening gravy and sauces.

Self-Raising Flour
This is low-protein, low-gluten white or wholemeal flour with a raising agent mixed in. The most usual raising agent added is baking powder or bicarbonate of soda.

Brown Flour
A flour with an 85% extraction rate – or a flour with 15% of the wholegrain extracted. Very little difference to a white flour except for the colour.

Spelt
An ancient variety of wheat with a rich nutty flavour. Today it is often included as part of a gluten intolerant diet as it is high in protein but

low in gluten. This makes it more easily digested particularly by those with a gluten intolerance.

Wholemeal

Essentially what it says. The entire wheat grain or berry is used to produce a 'wholemeal' flour. This is technically the same as 'wholewheat'.

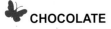 **BAKING POWDER**

A raising agent that is commonly used in cake-making. The powder is activated when liquid is added, producing carbon dioxide and forming bubbles that cause the mixture to expand. For this reason, it is important to get your cake mixture into the oven quickly once the 'wet' ingredients have been added to the 'dry' ingredients.

CHOCOLATE

The flavour of chocolate differs depending on the ingredients used and how it is prepared.

Real chocolate is made from cocoa and its ingredients include cocoa butter (an expensive part of the cocoa bean) and, in some cases, up to 5% vegetable fat.
Compound chocolate will have less cocoa and/ or more than 5% vegetable fat than real chocolate and therefore doesn't have the same fine qualities.

White Chocolate

This is chocolate made with cocoa butter, sugar, milk, emulsifier, vanilla and sometimes other flavourings. It does not contain any non-fat ingredients from the cocoa bean and has therefore an off-white colour. It has a mild and pleasant flavour and can be used to make chocolate mousse, panna cotta and other desserts.

Milk Chocolate

Sweet chocolate which normally contains a minimum of 20% cocoa solids (which includes cocoa and cocoa butter) and more than 12% milk solids. It is seldom used for baking, except for cookies.

Dark Chocolate

This is sweetened chocolate with a high content of cocoa solids and very little or no milk. It may contain up to 12% milk solids and is the chocolate most commonly used in desserts.

The amount of cocoa content tends to highlight the sweetness and quality of the chocolate. As a general rule of thumb if the content of cocoa solids is high the content of sugar is low, giving a rich, intense and more bitter chocolate flavour. For the sake of the recipes contained in this book we recommend using a good quality dark chocolate with a minimum 55-70% cocoa content.

 SUGAR

Today, refined sugar is the most popular type of sweetener and is made from sugar cane or sugar beet. The most obvious difference between the types of sugars is colour. When sugar has been extracted from the juice of the beet or cane plant, a strong tasting black syrup (known as molasses) remains. When white sugar is made, the molasses are entirely removed. The more molasses in brown sugar the stickier the crystals and the darker the colour, the stronger the flavour. The main sugars we use in baking are caster sugar and icing sugar.

Golden Caster Sugar: a fine sugar that is ideal for using in creamed sponge cakes.

Unrefined Demerara Sugar: darker in colour with a more intense flavour. With its coarse texture, it creates a lovely topping for cakes, cupcakes and crumbles.

Light Brown Soft Sugar: a popular choice for making fruit cakes and puddings where a rich, full flavour is required.

Dark Brown Soft Sugar: looks as its name suggests and has a richer flavour. It works well in cakes, gingerbread, pickles and chutneys.

VANILLA

Vanilla pods contain the seeds from the vanilla orchid plant. Real vanilla is expensive as each plant must be pollinated individually by hand. Only vanilla extract has the true flavour and aroma of vanilla pods. Vanilla essence is usually a synthetic vanilla flavouring and is cheaper than the natural extract. If you don't use the pods then I recommend using extract rather than essence for a better end result. 1 tsp of extract is the equivalent of one vanilla pod.

GELATINE

This is a colourless, tasteless and odourless setting agent. I use Bronze Leaf Gelatine and this must be soaked in very cold water until soft. It is dissolved in boiled liquid and then when cooled, it turns into a jelly-like form that is used to thicken and stabilise desserts such as jelly and panna cotta.

FRUIT

We can use many types of fruit in desserts and there is always room to experiment with different types of fruits across different recipes. But to get the best from fresh fruit, where possible, buy British when they are in season. Of course this also goes for savoury dishes too.

Tinned
The quality of many tinned fruits have improved in recent years but we always advocate using fresh if possible for the best quality results. But don't let that stop you if you have a tin in the cupboard as there are lots of recipes out there where tinned fruits can be a good substitute. However, you do need to watch the sugar content, especially with canned fruit preserved in syrup. For a healthier option, look out for canned fruit in juice with less added sugar.

Frozen
Frozen fruit is generally picked at the peak of ripeness and frozen quickly to lock in freshness and flavour with very little processing. It can be a good option especially when your favourite fruits are out of season and works well in ice creams and sorbets, though it still needs to be thawed before using if not in a baked product.

Equipment

SCALES

With baking, it's important to be precise with measurements so if possible electric scales are preferable. Any type of scale is fine but just take a little extra care with spring-loaded ones.

ICE CREAM SCOOPS

Of course a spoon will do but a scoop will help take the presentation of your dessert to another level. Plus they're much easier.

SPEED PEELER

Most people have a favourite peeler. My preference is the speed peeler and in my opinion the most effective.

STICK BLENDER

Very handy for making sauces, coulis, purees, smoothies and mixing flavours together.

MEASURING JUGS

Great for pouring and useful for rough quantities but for more precise measurements always use scales.

MICROPLANE ZESTER

The daddy of all zesters which is great for finely zesting all types of citrus fruits.

ROLLING PIN

A vital piece of kit especially for pastry making. There are no set rules for rolling pins but I prefer a traditional wooden one.

WHISK

Use this for the lighter jobs such as breaking up eggs, sifting flour and creaming softened butter.

ELECTRIC WHISK

A hand whisk is great, but an electric whisk is easier and more efficient. Don't be stubborn and try to hand whisk everything, life's too short!

FREE STANDING MIXER

A great investment for those who bake lots. They really can save a lot of time and mess as well as being very versatile. Usual attachments include a paddle, whisk and a hook.

RUBBER SPATULA

These are ideal for folding, scraping and of course licking! A useful tip is that the heatproof ones usually have a red handle whilst non-heatproof ones are usually white.

JUICER

Juicers are good for getting the maximum amount of juice out of fruit. A fork also works but not quite as efficiently.

GREASEPROOF PARCHMENT

Silicone (baking) paper works especially well. After baking, the paper peels away really easily. It does cost more than baking paper but it's worth it.

DOUGH SCRAPER

This is useful for folding mixtures, cutting pastry/dough and for scraping it off surfaces.

SIEVE

It's good to have a couple of sizes if possible, one for sifting and another for dusting but it's not essential.

KNIVES

I'm sure most people have their own favourite knives but useful additions when making desserts are a small serrated knife and a palette knife.

BAKING BEANS

Not to be confused with baked beans, baking beans are also called pastry weights, baking weights and pie weights. They are round balls, often ceramic, that are used in the blind baking of pastry. You can also use any dried items such as lentils or rice. Always remember to cover your pastry with baking paper before adding the beans. Essentially the beans will prevent the pastry from rising excessively and assist in the even distribution of heat.

BAKING TINS

The reason for so many failed cakes is that the size of tin was not quite right for the amount of mixture. Even a half-inch difference all round can often upset both the timing of a recipe and the finished size of the cake. It is therefore important to use the correct sized tin. In my recipes I usually try to keep to standard sizes that are readily available in most shops.

THE BASIC BAKING TINS:
Loaf tin
Loose-bottomed tin
Deep cake tin
Spring-form tin
Baking tray
Flan dish
Ramekin
Muffin tin

Indulgent Desserts

Chocolate Mousse with Honeycomb

When I asked people what recipe they would like to see in this book, at the top of most lists was my chocolate mousse. It's my bestseller and it's for all you chocoholics out there. The honeycomb adds a great texture so you can add as much or as little as you want. But please be extra careful when making it.

Makes 6 individual servings

TIP: Honeycomb can be made in advance and stored in an airtight container, though not in the fridge as it will soften.

CAUTION: The reaction between the bicarbonate of soda and caramel happens instantly and is slightly different every time. Always use a large, deep pan and keep your hands away from the caramel until it has cooled completely.

Chocolate Mousse	**Honeycomb**
250ml double cream	250g caster sugar
250g dark chocolate	100ml warm water
5 medium free range eggs	2 tsp bicarbonate of soda
100g caster sugar	For the method see page 140.

For the method see page 140.

The Mousse

- Whip the cream in a mixing bowl until just firm and place in the fridge.
- Melt the chocolate until smooth in a large bowl over a pan of simmering water (a bain-marie) making sure the base of the bowl does not touch the water.
- When the chocolate has melted but it is still hot, add the whipped cream and whisk until combined.
- In a separate bowl whisk the eggs and sugar until it has doubled in volume. Then add half of this mixture to the chocolate and gently fold together. When combined, repeat the process until the mix is light and the same colour throughout.
- Spoon the mixture into glasses or pots and place in the fridge for a minimum of 20 minutes.
- To serve, place the pieces of honeycomb on top of the mousse and enjoy.

Honey Crème Brûlée

A crème brûlée can be a thing of beauty or just a thing. By making sure you don't overheat the mixture and cooking it at a lower heat for longer, means that you will always get a fantastic result rather than overcooked scrambled eggs. For this recipe we used honey as the main flavour but be creative, anything – well almost anything – goes, as long as the fundamentals of how you cook it remain the same.

Makes approx. 5-6 individual servings

500ml double cream
10 medium free range egg yolks
150g honey
sprinkling of caster sugar

TIPS: When cooking the brûlée, the shallower the dish, the quicker the cooking time.

Caster sugar is easier to blow torch for the glaze as it melts faster due to the size of the sugar crystals; however if you would prefer more of a hard crunch use demerara. If you don't have a blow torch you can use a grill; however a blow torch does give a much better result.

CAUTION: After making the caramel disc it is vital to allow the glaze to cool completely before eating. Sugar reaches very high temperatures so be extra careful.

Method

- Preheat the oven to 100°C/212°F/gas mark ¼ to ½.
- In a bowl mix the egg yolks and honey. Set aside.
- In a thick-bottomed saucepan bring the cream to a boil.
- Remove from the heat and pour onto the egg and honey mix and whisk to combine.
- Return this mixture to a saucepan, and whilst continuously stirring on a low heat allow to thicken. When it coats the back of a spoon remove from the heat. Sieve this into a large jug to remove any lumps and pour into ramekins or heatproof portion size dishes.
- Place the ramekins onto a baking tray and put into the preheated oven for between 45 minutes and one hour. You will know they are ready when there is no wobble in the middle of the brûlée.
- Remove from the oven. Allow to cool and then place in the fridge to chill (preferably overnight) before glazing.

To Glaze

- Sprinkle a thin coating of caster sugar over the top of the custard and wipe the rim of the ramekin (this makes it easier to clean after).
- Using a blowtorch, burn the sugar until it has dissolved into a light caramel.
- Repeat this process a few times, until a nice caramel disc is formed.
- Allow to cool completely before serving.

Chocolate Fondant

The fondant has been the Achilles heel of many a Masterchef contestant as they strive for the perfect gooey centre breaking free from the light spongy crust. This is a fool-proof recipe, but timing is everything so keep a close eye on the fondants as they cook to get the perfect result.

TIP: For an even more visually impressive fondant, slightly melt a little white chocolate and roll it into a ball. Before baking carefully drop this into the filled moulds/ramekins and when you break it open you will amaze your guests as the chocolate filling will be two-toned.

Serves 6

250g salted butter
100g caster sugar
3 medium free range eggs
6 medium free range egg yolks
250g dark chocolate
50g plain flour

Method

- Preheat the oven to 180°C/350°F/gas mark 4.
- Whisk the eggs, additional yolks and sugar in a bowl until light and fluffy.
- In a separate large bowl gently melt the butter and chocolate over a pan of simmering water (a bain-marie) making sure the base of the bowl does not touch the water. When melted fold in the sieved flour, ensuring there are no lumps. Then fold in the whisked eggs and mix until combined.
- Pour the mixture into greased foil moulds or ramekins until approximately ¾ full. Place in the preheated oven for approximately 8-10 minutes. (If refrigerated and cooked from cold, these will take approximately 12-15 minutes at the same temperature.)
- They are ready when the top feels slightly firm to the touch. Allow to sit for 2 minutes.
- Then either eat straight from the mould/ramekin or turn out onto a plate. Ice cream, cream or crème fraîche provide a good accompaniment.

Jellies

Jelly is not just for children's parties, it's a versatile addition to many desserts and a standalone one in its own right. Have a go with different flavours and add some alcohol for a grown-up treat. But if you do, please don't forget to eat the jelly responsibly!

Each method makes 4-6 servings

TIP: The water element can be changed for a fruit juice or flavoured water if you wish to mix up the flavour. If you're layering fruit within any jelly make sure the final layer of jelly completely covers the fruit as this will prevent the air from getting to it and turning it mouldy.

Berry Jelly

500g raspberries or strawberries
500ml water
150g caster sugar
4 leaves of gelatine

- Soak the gelatine in cold water until soft.
- In a thick-bottomed saucepan, add the berries, sugar and water. Bring to a boil whisking the berries to break them down, then remove from the heat.
- Squeeze out the excess water from the gelatine and whisk into the berry mix until dissolved. If you would prefer a clearer jelly, pass the mixture through a sieve to remove the seeds.
- Using a ladle, portion into pots and chill in the fridge until firm.

Prosecco Jelly

1 bottle of prosecco
200g caster sugar
4 leaves of gelatine

- Soak the gelatine in cold water until soft.
- Place the sugar and one third of the prosecco into a thick-bottomed saucepan. Bring to the boil, and then remove from the heat.
- Squeeze out the excess water from the gelatine and whisk into the prosecco mix. Add the remaining prosecco.
- This jelly is great layered with fresh strawberries or raspberries. To do this you have to make sure the first layer of jelly is set properly and then add the fruit and pour on another layer of the jelly mix then set. You can repeat this as many times as you want as long as each layer of jelly is set individually.

Orange & Passion Fruit Trifle

A trifle can be a beautiful modern dessert, not just a boozy, sherry-laden, old-fashioned memory from your Grandma's Christmas table. I make this in shot glasses for a more delicate serving but there is nothing wrong with having a big bowl of it in the middle of the table for the whole family to dive into.

Serve in 1 large bowl, for 6-8 people

TIPS: Grate the zest of 1 orange into your chantilly cream to make your trifle extra orangey.

The fruit juice and alcohol can be exchanged for different flavours, so be experimental.

Compote
3 passion fruits
25g caster sugar
40ml orange juice

Jelly
250ml orange juice
250ml passion fruit juice
25g caster sugar
3 gelatine leaves
15ml Cointreau

Vanilla Custard
250ml double cream
5 medium free range egg yolks
50g caster sugar
¼ vanilla pod
For the method see page 132.

Extras
55g sponge fingers

Chantilly Cream
500ml double cream
¼ vanilla pod
80g caster sugar
zest of 1 orange (optional)
For the method see page 130.

The Jelly

- Soak the gelatine leaves in a bowl of cold water until soft.
- In a thick-bottomed saucepan add the orange juice, passion fruit juice and the sugar, bring to the boil and then remove from the heat.
- Squeeze the excess water from the gelatine leaves and then carefully add to the hot orange/passion fruit mixture.
- Add the Cointreau and whisk until the gelatine is fully dissolved.
- Lay the sponge fingers in the bottom of the bowl and carefully pour over the hot jelly mix. Cool for 15 minutes, then place in the fridge and allow to set.

The Compote

- Cut the passion fruit in half and scoop out the seeds. Add the seeds to a saucepan along with the sugar and the orange juice.
- Bring to the boil and then remove from the heat. Allow to cool.

Assembling The Trifle

- When the jelly has set, layer the thick, cold custard followed by the chantilly cream, top with the passion fruit compote and serve.

Panna Cotta with Raspberries

Panna Cotta is simply an Italian cooked cream. It has a daunting reputation but in reality it's very straightforward. Just add the right amount of gelatine and you'll be sure to achieve the perfect wobble.

Makes 6 individual portions

TIP: It's important to chill the mix until it just starts to set as this way the vanilla seeds hold all the way through the mix, rather than sinking to the bottom.

Panna Cotta	**Sauce**
250ml whole milk	250g raspberries
750ml double cream	50g caster sugar
100g caster sugar	50ml water
½ vanilla pod	
3 leaves of gelatine	

The Panna Cotta

- Soak the gelatine leaves in cold water until soft.
- In a thick-bottomed saucepan add the cream, milk, sugar and vanilla seeds and bring to the boil, stirring occasionally to make sure the sugar has dissolved. Remove from the heat.
- Take the gelatine leaves, squeeze out the excess water, and whisk into the cream mixture until dissolved. Pour the mixture into a shallow container and chill until it just starts to set.
- Remove from the fridge and pass through a sieve. Pour into moulds and place back in the fridge for a further 2-3 hours until fully set.

The Sauce

- In a large thick-bottomed saucepan, bring the caster sugar and water to the boil. When just boiled add the raspberries, blitz to a puree and then allow to cool.

Lemon Posset

Posset
250ml double cream
50g caster sugar
65ml lemon juice
zest of 1 lemon
25g sponge fingers

Lemon Syrup
50ml lemon juice
50g caster sugar
100ml water

Serves 2

Method

- To make the syrup, bring the water, lemon juice and sugar to the boil in a thick-bottomed saucepan.
- Place the sponge fingers in a medium-sized bowl and pour the mixture over the sponge fingers then allow to cool before layering to prevent the cream curdling.
- Whisk the cream, half of the lemon zest and sugar until it only just forms soft peaks, then add the lemon juice and whisk until a firm peak.

To Assemble

- Once the sponge/syrup mix is cool, take 2 glasses (wine glasses or small tumblers) and spoon a small amount of this mix into each glass, followed by an equal amount of the lemon cream. Repeat the process, and finely grate the remaining lemon zest over the top.
- Chill in the fridge for an hour and serve.

Gooseberry & Elderflower Fool

This is a light, timeless dessert perfect for summer, which is also quick and simple to prepare.

Serves 4-6

TIP: Serve with some biscotti or shortbread. Buy the gooseberries when in season and freeze in batches so you can use them all year round.

Compote
250g gooseberries topped and tailed
50g caster sugar
25ml water
25ml elderflower cordial

Fool
500ml double cream
100g caster sugar
50ml elderflower cordial
50ml white wine

The Compote

- In a thick-bottomed saucepan, add the gooseberries, sugar, water and elderflower cordial then bring to a boil stirring occasionally.
- When the gooseberries start to burst and break down, remove from the heat and allow to continue cooking in the residual heat for a few minutes. Place in the fridge to chill.

The Fool

- Whisk the cream and sugar until firm, then add the cordial and wine folding until combined.

To Serve

- In a glass, layer the cream and the compote alternating as often as you like. Place in the fridge to chill for about an hour and serve.

Peach & Amaretti Syllabub

4 ripe peaches
25g demerara sugar
50ml Amaretto liqueur
500ml double cream
100g caster sugar
50ml water
10 crushed Amaretti biscuits

Serves 4

Method

- Preheat the oven to 180°C/350°F/gas mark 4.
- Halve the peaches, remove the stones and place face-down on a tray pre-lined with greaseproof paper.
- Sprinkle with the demerara sugar, Amaretto and water. Place in the oven for 5-8 minutes, remove and allow to cool.
- Pour the syrup from the cooked peaches into a cup.
- Whisk the cream and caster sugar until thickened, then fold in the peach syrup and around ¾ of the crushed Amaretti biscuits.

To Serve

- For each serving layer some cream mix into a glass, followed by half a roasted peach, then repeat. Sprinkle with crushed Amaretti biscuits to finish.

Plum & Hazelnut Zabaglione

Zabaglione is a light custard which can be paired with a variety of fruits and accompaniments. In France it is referred to as a sabayon.

Serves 4

Base
6 firm plums
25g demerara sugar
50ml Marsala wine
25ml water
50g shelled hazelnuts

Zabaglione
10 medium free range egg yolks
150g caster sugar
25ml Marsala wine
150ml double cream

TIP: The zabaglione must be served as soon as it's made. It can also be glazed under the grill for a more caramelised flavour.

The Base

- Preheat the oven to 180°C/350°F/gas mark 4.
- Slice the plums in half, remove the stones and place face-down on a tray pre-lined with greaseproof paper. Sprinkle with the demerara sugar, water and Marsala, place in oven for 5-8 minutes, before allowing to cool.
- Pour the syrup from the cooked plums into a cup.
- Place the hazelnuts in the oven on a tray pre-lined with greaseproof paper for approximately 5 minutes until toasted. Allow to cool then crush slightly.

The Zabaglione

- In a bowl whip the double cream into firm peaks, then set aside.
- In a separate large bowl whisk the egg yolks and caster sugar over a pan of simmering water (a bain-marie) making sure the base of the bowl does not touch the water. Whisk until the mixture has tripled in volume and is a thick, frothy consistency.
- Remove from the heat, whisk in the Marsala, then fold in the whipped double cream to form the zabaglione.

To Serve

- Place 3 halves of plum into each plate or bowl and spoon the zabaglione over the top of them until they are covered. Sprinkle with some of the crushed hazelnuts and a drizzle of the syrup from the plum juices.

Meringue Tips

 meringue is nothing more than foam made from egg whites. We've talked about eggs in the ingredients section but it's also good to highlight that the fresher the egg the lighter the meringue will be.

Of course to make a meringue you have to separate the yolk from the white. I find that the simplest way to do this is to crack the egg and hold the shell halves over a bowl. Transfer the yolk back and forth between the halves, letting the white drop into the bowl and then transfer the yolk to another bowl to use in a variety of other recipes.

Cold eggs are easier to separate but conversely room temperature egg whites are easier and faster to beat and will achieve a little more volume. A good mixer is an important part in making a meringue as it needs to be mixed thoroughly. It is achievable by hand, but is a lot of hard work! Consistency plays a large part in how meringues are prepared.

Soft peaks are when egg whites form peaks with tips that curl over when the mixture is lifted. Stiff peaks are when egg whites form peaks with tips that stand straight when the mixture is lifted.

In short, when the meringue mix is done it won't be runny and you should be able to hold a spoonful of it upside down with none of it dropping off. Also, when you swirl a spoon through it the swirls should hold their shape indefinitely.

There are a few different methods to make meringue but for all the recipes in this book I use the Swiss meringue technique.

Method:
Place a bowl over a pan of boiling water (bain-marie), being careful that the bottom is not in contact with the water. Add the whites of four medium free range eggs and 200g of caster sugar to the bowl and heat gently until the sugar dissolves. Take this off the heat and whisk until thick and glossy. Then either spread the meringue over a tray covered with greaseproof paper or pipe little drops onto the tray using a piping bag.

Place in the oven for approximately 45-60 minutes, 100°C/212°F/gas mark ¼ to ½ until the meringues sound crisp when tapped underneath. Remove a small piece from the oven and allow to cool on the side for a minute, if it goes hard the meringue is ready. If not continue to cook.

Storing Meringue:
For recipes such as Lemon Meringue Pie (page 54) they are best served on the day that they are made. Left over baked meringue, such as that in the Strawberry Eton Mess recipe (page 48), can be reused but does need to be stored in an airtight container in a cupboard, not in the fridge.

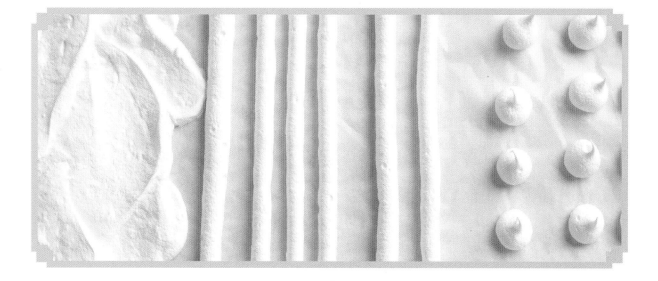

Baked Alaska

Believe it or not 1 February is Baked Alaska Day in the United States. Whilst this remains an institution in the US it has fallen by the wayside somewhat on these shores but let's bring it back with a bang and help your friends regain their lost youth with this show-stopping retro classic.

TIP: You can use whatever flavoured ice cream you want, so raid the freezers at your local supermarket or make your own to revive this childhood family favourite.

Sponge
250g salted butter
250g caster sugar
4 medium free range eggs
250g self-raising flour
25ml milk
1kg tub of your favourite ice cream

Meringue
9 medium free range egg whites
375g caster sugar
For the method see page 44.

Serves 6

The Sponge

- Preheat the oven to 160°C/325°F/gas mark 3.
- Cream together the butter and sugar until soft and pale in colour, then gradually add the eggs, mixing well until combined. Sieve in the flour followed by the milk and mix.
- Pour the mixture into two 8inch sandwich tins, pre-lined with greaseproof paper. Place in the oven for approximately 30 minutes until golden and springy to the touch.
- Remove from the oven and allow the cakes to cool.
- Once the cakes are cool and firm, slice a disc approximately 1cm thick from each sponge, and set the remaining sponge aside. Don't throw away the left over sponge as we will use this in the assembly of the Alaska.

To Build the Alaska

- Place 1 sponge disc into a clean 8inch sandwich tin pre-lined with greaseproof paper.
- Cut the left over sponge into strips the same depth as the tin, and line these around the sides of the tin.
- Spoon in the ice cream and fill until roughly 1cm from the top. Smooth the ice cream until flat and then place the second sponge disc on top, pushing down to compact.
- Place in the freezer for a couple of hours until frozen solid.

To Finish

- Increase the oven temperature to 200°C/400°F/gas mark 6. After you have made the meringue, remove the Alaska from the freezer. Release from the tin and place on a baking tray pre-lined with greaseproof paper. Liberally spread the meringue all over ensuring there are no gaps, especially at the base.
- Put the completed Alaska in the preheated oven for approximately 2-5 minutes or until the meringue is golden and serve straight away.

Strawberry Eton Mess

Eton mess is traditionally served at Eton College's annual cricket game against the students of Winchester College. This dessert was originally made with either strawberries or bananas mixed with ice cream or cream and the meringue was said to be a later addition. It can be made with many other types of summer fruit but strawberries are regarded as being the most traditional.

Serves 6-8

Strawberry Sauce
500g strawberries
50g caster sugar
50ml water

Chantilly Cream
500ml double cream
¼ vanilla pod
80g caster sugar
For the method see page 130.

Meringue
4 medium free range egg whites
200g caster sugar
For the method see page 44.

TIPS: This recipe will make lots of meringue, but if you use smaller quantities it is difficult to get the thick, glossy meringue consistency that you need. Store the extra in an airtight container.

The sauce can be frozen in small batches. So for an ultra-quick dessert all you need to do is defrost the sauce (if you warm the sauce it will split the cream), whip the cream, mix with any extra meringue pieces and assemble. Simple.

The Strawberry Sauce

- In a thick-bottomed saucepan add the caster sugar and water and bring to the boil.
- Add half of the strawberries, blitz to a puree then allow to cool.

The Mess

- Slice the remaining strawberries as thickly or thinly as you wish.
- Break up the meringues into bite-size pieces.
- Add the strawberries and around a third of the meringue pieces to the chantilly cream. This will leave lots of meringue for another day.
- Pour three quarters of the strawberry sauce over this mixture. Gently fold together and make a rippling effect with the sauce.
- Spoon the mixture into glasses and drizzle the remaining sauce over the top.
- Finally, sprinkle bits of crushed meringue to finish the mess and serve immediately.

Pavlova

The Pavlova is a meringue-based dessert named after the Russian ballet dancer Anna Pavlova. Its crisp crust and light, slightly gooey inside will make you leap for joy. For a topping, you can't go wrong with any mix of soft fruits and cream.

TIP: When whisking egg whites, make sure all of your equipment is extremely clean and grease free to ensure the best result.

Serves approx. 8

Chantilly Cream
500ml double cream
¼ vanilla pod
80g caster sugar

6 medium free range egg whites
200g caster sugar
10ml white wine vinegar
25g cornflour
30ml hot water
¼ vanilla pod (optional)

Extras
500g fresh seasonal berries

Method

- Preheat the oven to 150°C/300°F/gas mark 2.
- Whisk the egg whites until they form soft peaks. Gradually add one spoonful of sugar at a time and continue whisking until all of the sugar is added.
- Dissolve the cornflour in a small bowl with the hot water and vinegar, then slowly add to the egg whites and whisk until glossy and thick. Remove from the bowl and spoon onto parchment paper in a circular disc shape. Spoon the mix evenly and then place in the preheated oven for 30 minutes, and then turn down the heat to 100°C/212°F/gas mark ¼ to ½ for a further 90 minutes. Turn the oven off completely leaving the meringue inside until cool.

Chantilly Cream

- Pour the cream into a mixing bowl.
- Cut the vanilla pod in half lengthways with a sharp knife and scrape out half of the seeds. Add the seeds and the caster sugar to the cream. Whip the cream until it forms soft peaks.

To Serve

- When the meringue is cool, spoon the chantilly cream and the fresh berries on top and serve.

How to Make Pastry

At its most basic, pastry is a simple mixture of fat and flour bound together by some form of fluid, usually eggs or milk, to form a paste or dough.

There are lots of different types of pastry from puff to filo and shortcrust to choux.

For the most part, it's easier to buy certain types of ready-made pastry such as puff or filo as these tend to be good quality and can be time-consuming to make by hand.

I believe it's always worth making your own sweet and choux pastry as these are not only simple to prepare, but taste so much better when they're homemade.

Choux Pastry

This is used for profiteroles and éclairs. These measurements will make approximately 40 profiteroles or 20 éclairs.

250ml water
100g salted butter
150g plain flour
4 medium free range eggs
1 pinch of salt
1 pinch of caster sugar

Method

- Preheat the oven to 200°C/400°F/gas mark 6. Pre-line a baking tray.
- Melt the butter in a thick-bottomed saucepan, then add the water and boil. Whisk in the sieved flour, salt and sugar until the mixture forms a ball of dough and comes away cleanly from the sides of the pan.
- After 2 minutes, remove from the heat and continue to mix with a wooden spoon. Beat to remove some of the heat and then gradually add the eggs, until a soft pipeable paste is formed. Remove from the pan and place in a piping bag with a plain nozzle tube.
- These can be whatever size or shape you require, but make sure you leave sufficient gaps as the mixture will expand. Bake for 20-40 minutes depending upon the size or until golden-brown.

Sweet Pastry

125g room temperature salted butter
110g caster sugar
1½ medium free range eggs
250g plain flour

Method

- Cream together the butter and sugar until light and fluffy. Slowly add 1 beaten egg, followed by half of the other beaten egg and continue to mix. Sieve in the flour and mix until combined.
- On a lightly floured work surface knead the pastry by hand for 1 minute until it forms the consistency of slightly sticky dough. Portion into 2 blocks, wrap in cling film and chill in the fridge for a minimum of 2 hours.
- When the pastry is chilled, knead for 1 minute on a lightly floured surface and then using a rolling pin, roll until approximately ½ cm thick and large enough to cover the base and side of the dish.
- A simple way to line the dish without tearing the pastry is to use the rolling pin. Gently roll the remaining pastry around the rolling pin then lift it from the work surface and unroll the pastry so that it falls into position over the dish, centreing it as much as possible. Lightly push the pastry into the corners and trim any excess. Place this in the fridge for a further 10 minutes to relax the pastry.
- Preheat the oven to between 160°C/325°F/gas mark 3. The temperature may vary depending on the filling, so be sure to check.
- Cover the base with a few layers of cling film, and then fill with baking beans/rice. Bake for approximately 30 minutes until the base is golden. When you think the pastry is ready, remove the beans/rice. If it's not quite cooked pop back in the oven for 2-3 minutes without the beans/rice.
- There is generally no need to blind bake the base for something like an apple pie so use the same method to line the dish but also brush a little egg wash around the lip of the pastry to help seal the top and bottom layers. Then, again using a rolling pin, apply the top layer of pastry and crimp the edges by pinching the bottom layer of pastry with the top making sure to trim any excess pastry.

Lemon Meringue Pie

Lemon meringue pie reminds me of my childhood every time I eat it. The tartness of the lemon curd cuts through the sweetness of the light and fluffy meringue and the crisp pastry bottom adds the texture. If you haven't had it for a while I urge you to have a go, it might bring back some happy memories of your own.

TIP: Glazing the tart case with egg helps stop the lemon mix seeping into the pastry and making it soft.

Serves approx. 6-8

Lemon Mix
8 medium free range eggs
250g caster sugar
300ml lemon juice
500ml double cream

Meringue
5 medium free range egg whites
250g caster sugar
For the method see page 44.

Sweet Pastry
250g room temperature salted butter
250g caster sugar
3 medium free range eggs
500g plain flour
For the method see page 53.

The Lemon Mix

- After you have blind baked the tart case, turn the oven down to 90°C/194°F/gas mark ¼ and leave the door open to allow it to cool and reach this temperature.
- Whisk the eggs and sugar before adding the lemon juice, followed by the cream.
- Mix together and pass through a sieve. Pour into the pre-cooked tart case. Place in the oven for approximately 45 minutes to an hour until it is set. You will know when it is ready as it will not wobble in the middle.
- Remove from the oven and allow to cool, then chill in the fridge for 30 minutes.

To Assemble

- Increase the oven temperature to 200°C/400°F/gas mark 6.
- Prepare the meringue and once you have achieved stiff peaks, spoon the mixture onto the chilled lemon tart covering the pastry so it doesn't burn. Make peaks using a fork.
- Place in the oven for 3-5 minutes until golden. Remove and allow to cool.

Bramley Apple Pie

This is a simple, traditional and comforting dish for all the family. There is nothing fancy about apple pie, but who needs complicated when it tastes this good?

TIP: You can replace the apple with other fruits. If you are using berries, it's best to add some ground nuts as the pastry will absorb the juices and go soft.

Serves approx. 8

Apple Compote
1.5kg Bramley apples
40g salted butter
75g caster sugar
½ vanilla pod

Sweet Pastry
250g room temperature salted butter
225g caster sugar
500g plain flour
3 medium free range eggs
For the method see page 53.

Extras
1 medium free range egg
½ tsp of milk
1 tsp demerara sugar

Method

- Prepare the pastry and while it is chilling in the fridge, make the apple compote.
- Peel and dice the apples about 2cm in size and set aside. Melt the butter in a thick-bottomed saucepan and then add the vanilla pod (whole, not just the seeds), followed by half of the apples and all of the sugar. Cook on a medium heat, stirring occasionally for 3-4 minutes, before adding the remaining apples. Cook until the apples start to soften and then take off the heat. Remove the vanilla pod and put into a shallow container to cool quickly.
- Preheat the oven to 180°C/350°F/gas mark 4. Grease a 9inch baking tin/oven proof dish.
- Once the pastry is chilled, remove both pieces and place on a lightly floured surface. Separately knead each portion for 1 minute to bring into a ball, and then using a rolling pin, roll until ½cm thick. Keep lightly dusting the surface under the pastry with flour every few rolls to ensure that it doesn't stick.
- Place the rolling pin at the top of one of the portions and gently roll over the rolling pin. Place over the greased baking tin/oven proof dish.
- Push the pastry into the corners with your fingers and cut the excess from the rim of the dish and place this in the fridge for a further 10 minutes to relax the pastry.
- Once the apple compote is cool, fill the pastry and smooth over. Brush a little egg wash (one beaten egg with ½ tsp of milk) around the lip of the pastry. Roll the other piece of pastry on top and crimp the edges by pinching the bottom pastry with the top. Cut away excess pastry and egg wash the top. Sprinkle with a little demerara sugar and bake in the preheated oven until golden. Serve with fresh vanilla custard or cream.

Tarte Tatin

This is the ultimate French classic, which is basically an upside down tart. It's said it was originally conceived by mistake when baking an apple pie, but what a mistake! You can make your own puff pastry but in reality who has the time or the inclination? Shop-bought pastry is certainly of good enough quality to make a fabulous tarte tatin.

Serves 4-6

TIPS: Always place a tray underneath the dish when baking a tarte tatin. This will catch any caramel that may spill over whilst cooking.

Always use firm fruit, if not it will become too mushy during the baking process.

Caramel
200g caster sugar
50g butter
50ml double cream

Extras
1kg puff pastry
6-8 large bananas or 5-6 apples or 8-10 plums

The Caramel

- In a thick-bottomed saucepan on a medium heat gradually add sugar until a runny clear caramel is formed. Turn the heat right down and then stir in the butter. Don't worry if it looks like it has split.
- Add the cream and stir. When combined, pour into an 8inch round, deep oven proof baking dish and allow to cool.

The Tatin

- Preheat the oven to 200°C/400°F/gas mark 6.
- Lightly sprinkle the work surface with flour and roll out a disc of puff pastry about ½cm thick. You want it to be slightly larger than the top of the dish so that it overlaps by roughly 2cm. Discard the excess pastry.
- Slice the bananas into 4 pieces about 4cm high. (If you are using plums, slice in half and remove the stones. For apples, peel, core and cut into quarters.)
- Place the fruit face-down into the caramel coated dish, packing them together as tightly as possible. Place the pastry disc over the fruit and tuck any excess inside the dish to encase the fruit. Place in the preheated oven for 15-25 minutes until the pastry is golden brown. Carefully remove from the oven and allow to cool for 5-10 minutes.
- Place a plate over the top of the dish and quickly turn it over so the pastry is now on the bottom. Be very careful when doing this as the juice from the fruit and caramel will be extremely hot. Serve with vanilla ice cream or clotted cream.

Strawberry Sablé

The crisp, melt in your mouth sablé biscuits contrast perfectly with the cream and fresh seasonal strawberries to give a delicate but delicious dessert.

Makes 6 portions or 18 individual biscuits

TIP: The biscuits are very delicate so allow them to cool completely before assembling the dessert. Try not to overwork the pastry mix; it should be just combined and still soft. For the best results store the sablé pastry in the fridge overnight.

Biscuits
100g caster sugar
200g salted butter
250g plain flour
1 medium free range egg yolk

Chantilly Cream
500ml double cream
¼ vanilla pod
80g caster sugar
50g strawberry compote/jam

The Biscuit

- Cream together the butter and sugar until light and fluffy. Slowly add the egg yolk and continue mixing. Add the flour and mix until a soft dough is formed and store in the fridge for a minimum of 2 hours, but preferably overnight.
- Preheat the oven to 170°C/340°F/gas mark 3½.
- On a lightly floured surface, roll out the dough to a thickness of approximately 5mm. Using a 7cm cutter, cut into discs and then place on a baking tray pre-lined with greaseproof paper. Place this in fridge for 10 minutes.
- When chilled, bake for 12-15 minutes, until the sablés are a light sandy colour. Whilst still hot, lightly sprinkle with caster sugar before allowing to cool completely.

Chantilly Cream

- Pour the cream into a mixing bowl and add the vanilla seeds and caster sugar. Whip the cream until it forms firm peaks and then add the strawberry compote/jam.

To Assemble

- Place a small drop of cream on the plate and place a biscuit on top, this stops the biscuit from moving. Slice all of the strawberries so that they are the same height and spoon a dollop of cream in the centre of the biscuit. Place the strawberries around the outside of the biscuit enclosing the cream. Place another biscuit on top and repeat the process.
- Dust the last biscuit with icing sugar and place on the top. Serve with some fresh strawberries tossed in a strawberry sauce (page 48).

Bourbon Whiskey & Walnut Tart

Serves approx. 8

Walnut & Whiskey Mix
70g dark brown soft sugar
70g salted butter
2 medium free range eggs
1 pinch of salt
100g walnuts
40ml bourbon whiskey
150g golden syrup
20g black treacle

Sweet Pastry
125g room temperature salted butter
110g caster sugar
1½ medium free range eggs
250g plain flour

Method

- To make the pastry, cream together the butter and sugar until light and fluffy. Slowly add 1 beaten egg, followed by half of the other beaten egg and continue to mix. Add the sieved flour until combined.
- Place the pastry onto a lightly floured work surface. Knead it by hand for 1 minute until it forms the consistency of slightly sticky dough. Portion this into 2 blocks, wrap in cling film and place in the fridge for a minimum of 2 hours.
- Whilst this is chilling make the whiskey and walnut mix. Melt the butter, golden syrup and black treacle in a pan, and then remove from the heat. Beat the eggs in a separate bowl, and then add all the other remaining ingredients including the melted butter and sugar. Mix together and put to one side.
- Once the pastry is chilled, remove from the cling film onto a lightly floured surface. Knead this for 1 minute to bring into a ball, then get a rolling pin and roll it out until the pastry is approximately ½cm thick. Keep lightly dusting the surface under the pastry with flour every few rolls to ensure that it doesn't stick.
- Place the rolling pin at the top of the pastry and gently roll the pastry over the rolling pin. Lift and place over the greased baking tin/oven proof tart dish. Lightly push the pastry into the corners with your fingers and cut the excess pastry from the rim of the dish. Place this in the fridge for a further 10 minutes to relax the pastry.
- Preheat the oven to 160°C/325°F/gas mark 3.
- Place layers of cling film on top of the pastry and up the sides so that it is completely covered then fill this with baking beans/rice. Place on a baking tray in the preheated oven and bake for approximately 30 minutes or until the base is golden in colour.
- When the pastry base is ready, remove the baking beans and allow to cool. If it's not quite cooked, pop back in the oven for 2-3 minutes without the baking beans.
- When the pastry case is cooked, pour in the whiskey and walnut mix and place back in the oven for approximately 20-30 minutes or until the tart is set. Allow to cool completely before cutting.

Raspberry & Nectarine Tart

Sweet Pastry
125g room temperature salted butter
110g caster sugar
1½ medium free range eggs
250g plain flour
For the method see page 53.

Sponge
50g salted butter
60g caster sugar
1 medium free range egg
75g self-raising flour
¼ vanilla pod
60ml milk

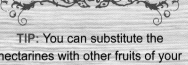

TIP: You can substitute the nectarines with other fruits of your choice such as pears or blackberries.

Apricot Glaze
75g apricot jam
25ml water

Extras
80g raspberry jam
2 nectarines (de-stoned)
125g fresh raspberries

Method

- To make the sponge, cream together the butter, sugar and vanilla seeds. Slowly add 1 beaten egg, followed by half of the other beaten egg, flour and milk, stirring in between each ingredient. Set aside.
- Once the pastry is chilled, remove from the cling film onto a lightly floured surface. Preheat the oven to 170°C/340°F/gas mark 3½. Knead the pastry for 1 minute to bring into a ball, and then roll it out until it is approximately ½cm thick. Keep lightly dusting the surface under the pastry with flour every few rolls.
- Place the rolling pin at the top of the pastry and gently roll the pastry over the rolling pin. Lift and place over the greased 9inch baking tin/oven proof tart dish.
- Push the pastry into the corners lightly with your fingers and cut the excess pastry from the rim of the dish. Place this in the fridge for a further 10 minutes to relax the pastry.
- In a clean bowl, beat the jam until smooth. Remove the pastry from the fridge, and spread the jam on the bottom followed by the sponge mix. Slice the nectarines in to 2cm thick wedges and place over the top followed by the raspberries. Place in the preheated oven and bake for 25-35 minutes until springy to the touch.
- To glaze, remove the tart from the tin and allow to cool. Boil the apricot jam and water and then brush over the tart. This will give the tart a nice shine. Store in the fridge and serve at room temperature.

Salted Caramel & Chocolate Tart

Sweet Pastry
125g room temperature salted butter
110g caster sugar
1½ medium free range eggs
250g plain flour
For the method see page 53.

Caramel
250ml double cream
125g caster sugar
25g salted butter

Chocolate Tart Mix
3 medium free range eggs
2 medium free range egg yolks
50g caster sugar
250g dark chocolate
100g salted butter

Method

- Prepare the pastry as per the method on page 53 and blind bake in a 9inch baking tin/oven proof tart dish at 160°C/325°F/gas mark 3 for approximately 30 minutes or until the base is golden in colour. When the tart base is almost cooked prepare the caramel.
- In a thick-bottomed saucepan add the sugar a little at a time until a golden runny caramel is formed, remove from the heat and whisk in the butter. Add a little of the cream and whisk, be careful as it may bubble away at this point. Once smooth, add the remaining cream. If lumpy, return to a low heat for a minute to warm the sauce slightly, then pass through a sieve and allow to cool.
- When the pastry base is ready, spread 100g or a couple of tablespoons of caramel sauce over the base of the tart.
- Place the chocolate and butter in a bowl, and suspend over a saucepan of simmering water (a bain-marie) do not allow the bowl to touch the water. When the mixture has melted, remove from the heat.
- Whisk the eggs, yolks and sugar until it has doubled in volume. Then fold half of this into the chocolate mix, followed by the remaining half. Pour this combined mixture over the caramel sauce to the lip of the tart and place in the oven for 15-20 minutes until it has just a slight wobble. Remove from the oven and allow to cool completely so the tart is firm before spreading another layer of caramel on top.

Orange & Almond Treacle Tart

Most Treacle Tart recipes use lemon, but I prefer orange because I think it compliments the almond. However if you do choose to use lemon, the acidity really cuts through the sweetness of the syrup.

Serves approx. 8

TIP: You can use a variety of different nuts such as hazelnuts or walnuts. Be sure to grind these first, using a food processor.

Sweet Pastry
125g room temperature salted butter
110g caster sugar
1½ medium free range eggs
250g plain flour
For the method see page 53.

Treacle Mix
1 medium free range egg
100g ground almonds
1 pinch of salt
120ml double cream
300g golden syrup
zest of 1 orange

The Treacle Mix

- Melt the butter and golden syrup in a pan, and remove from the heat. In a separate bowl, beat the eggs before adding the ground almonds. Mix well and then add the remaining ingredients, including the melted butter and golden syrup. Combine together and put to one side.

Assembling the Tart

- Once you have prepared and blind baked the pastry, pour in the treacle mix and place back in the oven for approximately 20-30 minutes at 160°C/325°F/gas mark 3. When the tart is set, remove from the oven and allow to cool completely before cutting. Serve with lemon mascarpone (page 131) and crushed Amaretti biscuits.

Profiteroles & Éclairs with Choux Pastry

Choux Pastry
250ml water
100g salted butter
150g plain flour
4 medium free range eggs
1 pinch of salt
1 pinch of caster sugar

Dark Chocolate Sauce
70g dark chocolate
100ml double cream

Extras
Cream of your choice,
see page 130 for options.

TIP: Make sure your pastry is cooked thoroughly and dry inside otherwise the pastry will go soft.

Choux Pastry

- Preheat the oven to 200°C/400°F/gas mark 6. Pre-line a baking tray.
- Melt the butter in a thick-bottomed saucepan, then add the water and boil. Whisk in the sieved flour, salt and sugar until the mixture forms a ball of dough and comes away cleanly from the sides of the pan.
- After 2 minutes, remove from the heat and continue to mix with a wooden spoon. Beat to remove some of the heat and then gradually add the eggs, until a soft pipeable paste is formed. Remove from the pan and place in a piping bag with a plain nozzle tube.
- When making éclairs, pipe long strips 10cm in length. For profiteroles, pipe 2cm diameter balls. Place in the oven for approximately 10-15 minutes or until golden and puffed up. Then turn down the heat to 170°C/340°F/gas mark 3½ to dry out the inside for a further 10 minutes or until hollow sounding when tapped underneath.

To Assemble

- I use crème légèr (page 130), but you can fill using any cream to suit your preference. To fill, insert a hole on the underneath of the choux bun, (2 for éclairs one each end) and then pipe the cream inside. For éclairs pipe into one hole until it comes out of the other hole, this way you know it's full with cream. If you don't have a piping bag, slice the choux pastry lengthwise and carefully spoon in the cream.
- Place chocolate in a bowl. Pour the cream in a saucepan and bring to the boil and then pour over the chocolate. Whisk until completely melted and allow to cool slightly so it becomes a thick, coating consistency. (If you are using shop-bought sauce, simply warm and allow to cool to form a similar thick consistency.) Place the top of the choux bun in the sauce and allow the excess to drip off, turn over and place on a baking tray or cooling rack to set, ideally somewhere cool for 15 minutes.

Bramley Apple Crumble

If the humble crumble was a human it would probably have been knighted by now as it really is a national treasure! Despite most school canteen desserts being decidedly terrible the crumble even seemed good back then. I promise that despite these memories this one is even better!

TIP: Sprinkle some demerara sugar on top of the crumble before cooking for that extra crunch.

Apple Compote
1kg Bramley apples
25g salted butter
50g caster sugar
¼ vanilla pod

Crumble Topping
200g plain flour
100g room temperature salted butter
25g caster sugar
½ medium free range egg

The Apple Compote

- Peel and dice the apples about 2cm in size and set aside.
- Melt the butter in a thick-bottomed saucepan and then add the quarter vanilla pod (whole not just the seeds) followed by the sugar and half of the apples. Cook on a medium heat, stirring occasionally for 3-4 minutes, before adding the remaining apples. Cook until the apples start to soften and then remove from the heat. Take out the vanilla pod, and then put into a baking dish and set aside.

The Crumble

- Preheat the oven to 180°C/350°F/gas mark 4.
- Place the flour and butter into a mixing bowl and rub together until it forms a crumb. Add the sugar and mix again. Beat the egg and add half to the mixture, continue to mix quickly until just combined.
- Cover the apples with a 1cm layer of crumble topping, and then place in the preheated oven for approximately 15-25 minutes or until golden. A longer cooking time is needed for a thicker crumble topping. Serve with some vanilla custard.

Puddings & More...

Brioche Bread & Butter Pudding

500g loaf of sliced brioche
100g salted butter
1litre milk
10 medium free range eggs
200g caster sugar
1 vanilla pod
50g walnuts
50g dark chocolate
Apricot jam to glaze

Serves 8-10

Method

- Preheat the oven to 160°C/325°F/gas mark 3.
- Butter both sides of the bread and set aside. Whisk the eggs and caster sugar together and using a thick-bottomed saucepan, bring the milk and vanilla pod to the boil. When boiled, pour over the eggs and sugar and mix to combine. Pass through a sieve and set aside.
- Cover the base of an 8inch tin with the bread, and alternate the layers with small pieces of chocolate and walnuts. Half fill the tin with the egg mixture, covering the bread, allowing it to absorb the liquid. Continue to layer the bread until you reach the top. Add the remaining custard, to within 1cm from the top of the tin.
- Sprinkle with walnuts and demerera sugar, and place in the preheated oven for 25-35 minutes.
- To finish, you can brush the pudding with warm apricot jam.

Summer Pudding

1.5kg frozen summer berries
250g caster sugar
zest of 1 orange
½ vanilla pod
400g loaf of sliced brioche

Makes a 1litre sized bowl, serves 8-10

Method

- Bring the fruits, sugar, orange zest and vanilla pod to the boil. Cook until the fruits are defrosted and become slightly soft, then drain the juice through a sieve into a bowl. Be sure not to drain them dry, to keep some moisture.
- Briefly soak both sides of the bread in the hot liquid, and place around the sides of the bowl so that no gaps are left. Add the drained fruit and pack in well. Soak more bread in the hot liquid and place over the top, so that all the fruits are now encased in bread.
- The pudding must now be weighed down to compress it so the juice bleeds into the bread and becomes firm. You can do this by sitting something heavy on top of the pudding, and placing it in the fridge for a minimum of 4 hours. When ready to serve, place a plate on top of the bowl and quickly turn upside down and place on the table, then carefully ease the bowl off and hopefully the pudding will come out in one piece! Drizzle with the remaining juice and serve with clotted cream or crème fraîche.

Rice Pudding

TIPS: Wash the rice first under cold water to remove excess starch and prevent it from clumping together. To flavour your rice pudding, replace the 25g of sugar with 40g of your favourite jam or marmalade.
If you are serving the rice pudding cold, use 100g of pudding rice instead.

500ml milk
250ml double cream
135g pudding rice
½ vanilla pod
zest of half an orange
25g salted butter
25g caster sugar
200g condensed milk

Method

- In a thick-bottomed saucepan add the milk, cream, vanilla seeds and orange zest and bring to the boil.
- Add the rice, reduce the heat and simmer gently, stirring occasionally to prevent it sticking and burning on the bottom. Continue until the rice is soft.
- Remove from the heat and stir in the butter, sugar and condensed milk, serve straight away with fresh fruit or roasted nuts.

Tiramisu

Cream
500g mascarpone
250ml double cream
3 medium free range eggs
50g caster sugar

Coffee Syrup
500ml water
125g caster sugar
10g instant coffee

Extras
100g sponge fingers
sprinkling of cocoa powder

TIP: Add 25ml of Tia Maria or coffee liqueur if you want to give it more of a kick!

Method

- For the syrup, boil the sugar and water together in a thick-bottomed pan, then add the coffee. Remove from the heat and set aside.
- Suspend a bowl over a pan of simmering water and whisk the three egg yolks and half of the sugar together until pale and aerated, then set aside.
- In a separate bowl, whisk the double cream until if forms soft peaks, then beat the mascarpone to make it softer and add to the cream until combined.
- In a clean bowl, whisk the three egg whites until firm, then gradually add the remaining sugar and whisk until firm.
- Fold all components together, the yolks, whites and mascarpone cream, and mix until combined.
- Soak the sponge fingers in the coffee syrup and spoon half on the bottom of a dish, followed by half the cream, and repeat until complete. Dust with a light coating of cocoa powder on top and serve.

Sticky Toffee Pudding

This pudding is a great British institution. It is loved by pretty much everyone and is comfort food at its finest. This is a recipe that will brighten up any cold, miserable day and give you a warm glow inside and out.

8inch square baking tin

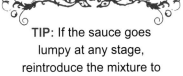

TIP: If the sauce goes lumpy at any stage, reintroduce the mixture to a low heat and stir until smooth, and pass through a sieve.

Sponge
80g salted butter
275g dark brown soft sugar
3 medium free range eggs
325g self-raising flour
½ tsp bicarbonate of soda
1 tsp baking powder

Sauce
125g salted butter
500g caster sugar
500ml double cream

Date Purée
250g dates (without stones)
250ml water

The Date Purée

- In a thick-bottomed saucepan, add the dates and water and simmer on a low heat until the dates are soft. Then blitz to a purée and allow to cool.

The Sponge

- Preheat the oven to 170°C/340°F/gas mark 3½.
- Cream the butter and the sugar until light and fluffy. Add the eggs one at a time, continuing to mix well.
- Sieve in the dry ingredients (flour, bicarbonate of soda and baking powder) and gently fold into the mix, then add the date purée. Mix until combined and then spoon into the pre-lined cake tin and smooth until even. Place in the oven for approximately 30-40 minutes until springy to the touch.

The Sauce

- In a thick-bottomed saucepan add the sugar a little at a time until a golden runny caramel is formed, remove from the heat and whisk in the butter. Add a little of the cream and whisk, be careful as it may bubble away at this point. Once smooth, add the remaining cream.
- Serve the pudding warm and pour the sauce liberally over the top. Perfect with ice cream or if you would like to cut through the sweetness, serve with crème fraîche.

Cherry Black Forest

Cherry Sauce
200g cherries
50g caster sugar
25ml water

Cream
250g mascarpone
25g caster sugar

Serves 4

Dark Chocolate Sauce
170g dark chocolate
200ml double cream

You can either use shop-bought brownies, or see page 110 for the method.

The brownie quantity will make double the amount that you need, so either halve the amount, or enjoy separately! Bake the brownies, and allow to cool before assembling.

Cherry Sauce

- Remove the stones from the cherries. In a thick-bottomed saucepan add the sugar, water and the cherries and bring to the boil. Cook for 1 minute so that the cherries are warmed through but still firm. Remove from heat and allow to cool completely.
- If you wish to make more of a cherry compote, blitz the cherries with the sugar syrup.

Cream

- Place the chocolate in a bowl, and suspend over a saucepan of simmering water (a bain-marie) do not allow the bowl to touch the water.
- When the chocolate has completely melted, mix in the cream and set aside.
- Beat the mascarpone with the sugar and half of the chocolate sauce until smooth and all one colour.
- To assemble, dice the brownie into bite-sized pieces, and either in individual glasses or a large bowl, layer the brownie, cream, cherry sauce and rest of the chocolate sauce, or you can present the brownie whole as pictured topped with the cream and cherries.

Bitter Chocolate Semi Freddo

Stage One
200ml double cream
300g dark chocolate

Stage Two
750ml double cream
100g honey
6 medium free range egg yolks
50g caster sugar

Stage One

Serves 10-12

- Break the chocolate into small pieces, and place into a bowl. Pour the cream into a saucepan and bring to the boil, then pour over the chocolate and whisk until completely melted.

Stage Two

- Place the honey, egg yolks and sugar in a bowl.
- In a thick-bottomed saucepan bring the cream to a boil then pour over the egg mixture and whisk.
- Transfer this mixture back to the saucepan and continue to thicken on a low heat whisking all the time. It will be ready when it just coats the back of a spoon.
- Pass this through a sieve onto the chocolate mixture and allow to chill in the fridge for around 30 minutes or until it just starts to firm up but remains a pouring consistency.
- Remove from the fridge and pour into an 8inch round cake tin pre-lined with greaseproof paper.
- Place in the freezer until frozen, preferably overnight.
- To serve, remove from the freezer and guide a hot knife around the edge of the tin until the semi freddo becomes loose.
- Place a plate on top of the tin, and turn the whole thing upside down. Using a hot knife, slice wedges and serve with a warm chocolate sauce and fresh raspberries or Oreo's.

What to know about Cheesecakes…

A good cheesecake is much, much more than a retro eighties throwback. It is a beautiful, versatile dessert which is perfect for those experimental dessert makers in terms of flavourings, toppings and even bases.

There are lots of versions for the cheesecake mix. I tend to use Philadelphia for my main cream cheesy element but for lower calorie cheesecakes you can obviously use less butter in the base and low fat cream cheese/cream varieties.

There are two main types of cheesecake: baked and non-baked. Arguably the most well-known baked version is the New York style cheesecake.

Whether baked cheesecake should be classified as a cake, a custard, a torte, or something else remains a matter of debate.

According to that fountain of all knowledge Wikipedia the early Greeks, from whom the form originates, considered it a cake. Some modern authors point to the presence of many eggs, the sole source of leavening, as proof that it is a torte. Others claim that the separate crust, the soft filling, and the absence of flour prove that it is a custard pie. But whatever it is classed as, it is simple to make and best of all tastes delicious.

For set cheesecakes, a spring-form tin is a really useful piece of kit. Plain Digestive biscuits work well as a base but you can also use other types of biscuits like cookies or bourbons to form different flavoured bases.

Banoffee Cheesecake

This is not the traditional way of building and serving a cheesecake and could be more suitably described as a deconstructed banoffee cheesecake. Serving it this way allows you to adjust each element to your taste and is perfect for a dinner party as you can pre-prepare everything beforehand and simply assemble before serving.

Serves 4-6

TIP: Do not add all the bananas at once or the caramel will cool too quickly and the sauce will become lumpy.

CAUTION: Use a large pan and a long-handled wooden spoon for the sauce as when you add the condensed milk it will bubble rapidly and is prone to spitting.

Banoffee Sauce
200g or 2 large bananas peeled & finely sliced
150g caster sugar
100g condensed milk

Banoffee Cream
250g Philadelphia
250ml double cream
70g caster sugar
¼ vanilla pod

Base
100g Digestive biscuits

Banoffee Sauce

- Pre-slice the bananas and place them somewhere close to hand.
- In a thick-bottomed saucepan gradually add the sugar, stirring occasionally until dissolved. When this becomes a light caramel in colour remove from the heat, stirring continuously whilst adding the condensed milk.
- Beat half of the bananas into the caramel until it softens and allow to sit for 5 minutes.
- Add the remaining bananas, stir and allow to cool completely. Store in the fridge.

Banoffee Cream

- Whisk the sugar, Philadelphia, cream and vanilla seeds until smooth and of a thick piping consistency. Store in the fridge.

The Base

- Blitz the Digestive biscuits in a food processor, or pop them into a freezer bag and gently crush with a rolling pin until they become a fine crumb.

To Serve

- Place some crushed biscuits onto a plate. Then, using a very large hot spoon, quenelle the cream mix on top of the biscuits. Pour the sauce over the top and around. For a final flourish, add a sprinkling of the biscuit crumb. Or construct in a glass as pictured.

Afternoon Tea & Cakes

Carrot & Roasted Walnut Cake

This recipe makes a deliciously moist cake, and it's worth taking that extra five minutes to roast the walnuts as it really brings out their flavour and adds a fabulous crunch. This is yet another firm favourite with my regulars. I'm not a tea drinker but I'm reliably informed that this cake provides the perfect accompaniment.

TIP: Grate your carrots finely, as this will make your cake lovely and moist.

Makes 2 x 23cm (9inch) round cakes

Cream Cheese Icing
600g icing sugar
200g Philadelphia
125g room temperature salted butter
zest of 1 orange

Extras
50g roasted walnuts

Sponge
250g salted butter
300g caster sugar
4 medium free range eggs
350g self-raising flour
1 tsp baking powder
½ tsp ground cinnamon
1 tsp bicarbonate of soda
500g grated carrot

The Sponge

- Preheat the oven to 160°C/325°F/gas mark 3.
- Line the cake tins with non-stick parchment/greaseproof paper.
- Cream the butter and sugar until light and fluffy. Add the eggs slowly one-by-one and mix until fully combined.
- In a separate bowl, add the flour, cinnamon, baking powder and bicarbonate of soda. Sieve these into the mixture and continue mixing until just combined. Add the carrot and mix for a further 2 minutes.
- Divide into the 2 pre-lined cake tins and smooth the mixture with the back of a spoon until even. Place into the preheated oven for approximately 45 minutes. When the cake is golden and springy to the touch, remove from the oven and allow to cool.

The Icing

- Cream the butter and sieved icing sugar together, then add the Philidelphia and orange zest. Mix until smooth.

To Serve

- Lightly roast the walnuts in the oven for around 5 minutes, then allow to cool.
- Cover one of the sponges with half the icing, then place the remaining sponge on top, covering that with the remaining icing. Finish with the roasted walnuts.

Zingy Lemon Drizzle Cake

Sponge
250g salted butter
250g caster sugar
4 medium free range eggs
250g self-raising flour
1 tsp baking powder
zest of 3 lemons
100ml milk

Icing
350g icing sugar
juice of 2 lemons
zest of 1 lemon

10inch square cake tin

Syrup
juice of 2 lemons
25g caster sugar
25ml water

TIP: Sprinkle some blueberries or toasted nuts on top of the icing if you want to jazz it up a bit.

The Sponge

- Preheat the oven to 170°C/340°F/gas mark 3½.
- Cream together the butter, sugar and lemon zest. Slowly add the eggs and sieve in the flour and baking powder. Now add the milk and mix until combined. Place in the pre-lined cake tin and bake for approximately 30-40 minutes until golden and springy to the touch. Allow to cool slightly.

The Syrup

- Boil together the lemon juice, sugar and water for 1 minute, and then brush over the cake and allow to cool completely before icing.

The Icing

- Place the sieved icing sugar and lemon zest in a bowl and add enough lemon juice to make a thick icing which coats the back of a spoon and is easily spreadable. The amount of lemon juice to add will all depend on how juicy the lemons are. Once ready, spread over the top of the cake and allow to set.

Mocha Cake

Sponge
300g salted butter
375g caster sugar
7 medium free range eggs
450g self-raising flour
2 tsp baking powder
100ml milk
10/20ml coffee essence
200g dark chocolate

Icing
500g icing sugar
250g salted butter
10ml coffee essence

Method

- Preheat oven to 170°C/340°F/gas mark 3½.
- Place the chocolate in a bowl, and suspend over a saucepan of simmering water, do not allow the bowl to touch the water, and leave to melt. Cream together the butter and sugar. Slowly add the eggs and continue to mix.
- Add the flour and baking powder, mix, and then add the milk, coffee essence, and the melted chocolate. Place in a pre-lined cake tin and bake for approximately 30-40 minutes until springy to the touch. Allow to cool.
- In a separate bowl cream together the sieved icing sugar and butter, and then add the coffee essence to taste. When the cake is cool you can either ice as it is, or cut in half and layer with the icing.

Orange & Poppy Seed Cake

Sponge
400g salted butter
400g caster sugar
5 medium free range eggs
400g self-raising flour
2 tsp baking powder
zest of 3 oranges
35g poppy seeds
200ml milk

2 x 9inch round cake tin

Orange Syrup
juice of 3 oranges
25g caster sugar

Cream Cheese Icing
600g icing sugar
200g Philadelphia
125g room temperature salted butter
zest of 1 orange

The Sponge

- Preheat the oven to 170°C/340°F/gas mark 3½ .
- Cream together the butter, sugar, poppy seeds and orange zest. Slowly add the eggs before the flour and baking powder, mix, and then add milk.
- Line the cake tins with greaseproof paper and divide the cake mix between the 2 cake tins then bake for approximately 25-35 minutes until golden and springy to the touch. Allow to cool.

The Syrup

- Boil together the orange juice and sugar to make a syrup, then brush over the cakes and allow to cool completely before icing.

The Icing

- Cream the butter and sieved icing sugar together, then add the Philadelphia and orange zest, beating until smooth. Layer the icing between both sponges and on top, then cover the sides. Sprinkle some poppy seeds on top for decoration.

Chocolate & Raspberry Cake

Sponge
300g salted butter
375g caster sugar
7 medium free range eggs
450g self-raising flour
1 tsp baking powder
100ml milk
200g dark chocolate

Icing
750g icing sugar
375g salted butter
100g dark chocolate

Extras
350g fresh raspberries

4 x 8inch round cake tins

Method

- Preheat the oven to 170°C/340°F/gas mark 3½.
- Place the chocolate in a bowl, and suspend over a saucepan of simmering water (a bain-marie) do not allow the bowl to touch the water, leave to melt.
- Cream together the butter and sugar. Slowly add the eggs and mix. Now add the flour and baking powder, and mix, before adding the milk and melted chocolate. Divide the mixture into the 4 pre-lined cake tins then bake for approximately 15-20 minutes until springy to the touch. Allow to cool.
- For the icing, melt the chocolate in the bain-marie method above. Cream together the sieved icing sugar and butter, and then add the melted chocolate. When the cake has cooled, layer each sponge with the icing and fresh raspberries including the top.

Madagascan Vanilla Victoria Sponge

Sponge	Vanilla Syrup	Icing	Extras
200g salted butter	50ml water	375g icing sugar	1 jar of raspberry or
250g caster sugar	50g caster sugar	190g salted butter	strawberry jam
5 medium free range eggs	1 used vanilla pod	½ vanilla pod	
300g self-raising flour		20ml milk	2 x 8inch round cake tins
½ vanilla pod			
60ml milk			

The Sponge

- Preheat the oven to 170°C/340°F/gas mark 3½.
- Cream the butter, sugar and vanilla seeds together before slowly adding the eggs and continue to mix. Add the flour, combine, and then add milk.
- Divide the mix into the 2 pre-lined cake tins and bake for approximately 20-25 minutes until springy to the touch. Allow to cool. Meanwhile, make the vanilla syrup by boiling all the ingredients together. Remove the sponge from the tins and brush the syrup over the cakes.

To Serve

- Cream together the sieved icing sugar, butter and vanilla seeds, then add the milk, and set the icing aside. When the cakes have cooled, put one on a plate and spread a layer of jam followed by the icing. Place the remaining sponge on top and dust lightly with icing sugar. Decorate with fresh raspberries or strawberries.

'Caprese' Chocolate & Almond Cake

This is a traditional Italian chocolate and almond cake named after the island of Capri from which it originates. As it's made without flour, it's perfect for people following a gluten free diet.

250g salted butter
250g caster sugar
250g ground almonds
5 medium free range eggs
100g dark chocolate
15g flaked almonds

Method

- Preheat the oven to 170°C/340°F/gas mark 3½. Pre-line an 8inch cake tin.
- Place the chocolate in a bowl, and suspend over a saucepan of simmering water (a bain-marie) do not allow the bowl to touch the water, allowing to melt. Cream together the butter and sugar, and then mix in the eggs, followed by the ground almonds and melted chocolate.
- Spoon into the cake tin and smooth. Sprinkle with flaked almonds, and place in the preheated oven for approximately 30-40 minutes until firm to the touch. Allow to cool. Serve with dark chocolate sauce and mascarpone cream.

Apple & Plum Cake

Sponge
200g salted butter
250g caster sugar
5 medium free range eggs
300g self-raising flour
60ml milk
2 apples
3 plums

Vanilla Syrup
2 tbsp water
30g caster sugar
¼ vanilla pod

TIP: I like to use Braeburn apples, however you can use any sweet or tart apple you prefer. Do not slice the fruit too thin or it will burn before the cake cooks.

Method

- Preheat the oven to 170°C/340°F/gas mark 3½.
- Slice the apples into wedges, removing the core. There should be approximately 8-12 wedges per apple, depending on size. Slice the plums into 4-6 wedges depending on size and set aside.
- Pre-line a 10inch square cake tin. Cream together the butter and sugar, and then slowly add the eggs. Add the flour, mix until combined before adding the milk. Spoon into the cake tin and smooth evenly.
- Place the apples on top of the cake mix, this can be in a particular design or just random, then the plums on top. Bake for 25-35 minutes or until golden and springy to the touch. Allow to cool. Meanwhile make the vanilla syrup by boiling all of the ingredients together, and brush over the cake to finish.

Red Velvet Cake

This is a visually stunning cake which is especially popular in the United States, but has also become much loved over this side of the pond.

TIP: If you use natural food colouring you will need to use a lot more than normal to gain a deep red colour.

Sponge
400g salted butter
400g caster sugar
5 medium free range eggs
350g self-raising flour
50g cocoa powder
2 tsp baking powder
50ml milk
76ml red food colouring

Cream Cheese Icing:
600g icing sugar
200g Philadelphia
125g room temperature salted butter

2 x 9inch round cake tin

The Sponge

- Preheat the oven to 170°C/340°F/gas mark 3½.
- Cream together the butter and sugar before slowly adding the eggs. Mix in the sieved flour, cocoa and baking powder, then add the milk and red colouring. Divide the cake mix between the 2 pre-lined cake tins and bake for approximately 25-35 minutes until golden and springy to the touch. Allow to cool.

The Icing

- Cream the butter and sieved icing sugar together and then add the Philadelphia, beat until smooth. Layer the icing between both sponges and then on top, dust with cocoa powder.

Vanilla Cupcakes

TIP: This is a good base recipe for any flavour cupcake, you can add flavourings and colourings to the sponge and icing to taste. For example, to make raspberry and almond cupcakes, I would add 100g of raspberries into the sponge, and 60g into the icing and gently fold in. Then garnish with some lightly roasted almonds.

Makes approx. 15-20

Sponge	Icing
200g salted butter	375g icing sugar
250g caster sugar	190g salted butter
5 medium free range eggs	½ vanilla pod
300g self-raising flour	20ml milk
½ vanilla pod	
60ml milk	

Method

- Preheat the oven to 170°C/340°F/gas mark 3½. Line 2 x 12 cupcake tins with cupcake paper cases.
- Cream together the butter, sugar and vanilla seeds. Slowly add the eggs, followed by the sieved flour, milk and continue to mix.
- Spoon the mixture into each paper case until they are half full and bake for approximately 20-25 minutes or until springy to the touch. Allow to cool.
- To make the icing, cream together the sieved icing sugar, butter and vanilla seeds. Add the milk and beat until light and fluffy. Make sure the cupcakes have cooled by the time you want to ice them. You can garnish with your favourite nuts, fruit or chocolate.

Chocolate, Caramel & Walnut Cupcakes

Sponge
200g salted butter
250g caster sugar
5 medium free range eggs
300g self-raising flour
150g dark chocolate
60ml milk

Icing
375g icing sugar
190g salted butter
handful of walnuts
40g dark chocolate

Caramel
125ml double cream
125g caster sugar
25g salted butter

Makes approx. 15-20

The Caramel

- In a thick-bottomed saucepan, add the sugar a little at a time until a golden runny caramel is formed, remove from the heat and whisk in the butter. Add a little of the cream and continue to whisk, be careful as it may bubble away at this point. Once smooth, add the remaining cream. If it becomes lumpy, return to a low heat for 1 minute to warm the sauce slightly, then pass through a sieve.

Method

- Preheat the oven to 170°C/340°F/gas mark 3½ and line 2 x 12-hole cupcake tins with cupcake paper cases.
- Place the chocolate in a bowl, and suspend over a saucepan of simmering water (a bain-marie) do not allow the bowl to touch the water, until the chocolate has melted.
- Cream together the butter and sugar. Slowly add the eggs, sieved flour, milk and then mix. Add the melted chocolate and mix until combined. Spoon the mix into the cupcake cases until about half full and bake for approximately 20-25 minutes until springy to the touch. Allow to cool.
- Toast a handful of walnuts by placing them in the oven on a baking tray for 3-5 minutes until golden, then allow to cool.
- To make the icing melt the chocolate using the bain-marie method above. Cream together the icing sugar and butter until light and fluffy. Mix in the melted chocolate. When the cakes have cooled, spoon the icing on top, followed by a small amount of caramel and toasted walnuts.

Cinnamon & Pumpkin Cupcakes

Sponge
200g salted butter
250g caster sugar
5 medium free range eggs
300g self-raising flour
1 tsp ground cinnamon
100g pumpkin
½ vanilla pod
60ml milk

Icing
375g icing sugar
190g salted butter
½ vanilla pod
20ml milk

Extras
100g pumpkin seeds

Makes approx. 15-20

Method

- Preheat the oven to 170°C/340°F/gas mark 3½. Line 2 x 12 cupcake tins with cupcake paper cases.
- Dice the pumpkin into 5-8mm chunks. Cream together the butter, sugar and vanilla seeds. Slowly add the eggs and continue to mix. Add the sieved flour, cinnamon and diced pumpkin and mix again. Finish by slowly adding the milk, and mixing until all ingredients are combined. Spoon the mix into paper cases until about three quarters full and bake for approximately 20-25 minutes until springy to the touch. Allow to cool.
- Toast the pumpkin seeds by placing them in the oven on a baking tray for 3-5 minutes until golden, and then allow to cool.
- To make the icing, cream together the sieved icing sugar, butter and vanilla seeds, and then add the milk, beat until light and fluffy. When the cakes have cooled, spoon the icing on top and add a sprinkling of pumpkin seeds.

How To Decorate Cupcakes

The cupcake revolution has been gathering for some years and there are now classes all over the country on how to make, decorate and bling up your cupcake.

There is nothing more satisfying than making a beautifully decorated cupcake and showing off your creativity to friends. But sometimes, in the sanctuary of your own kitchen without the pressure of an audience, it's also nice just to make a lovely simple icing, pile it high and eat it there and then.

The key is the type of icing you choose. The simplest and arguably still the best is a buttercream icing. The most basic method, this is made from butter and icing sugar with a touch of liquid (milk, melted chocolate, fruit juice for example). You can add a host of extra flavourings such as orange zest, vanilla extract, even your favourite liqueur and of course a colouring of your choice to liven it up.

You can pipe it, smear it, layer it or mould it. Look online for some inspiration and most of all use your imagination and be creative. After all cupcakes should be fun as well as delicious!

Moreish Oaty Flapjacks

In my opinion the best flapjacks are soft, sticky, chewy and highly moreish. Here's my recipe, which ticks all these boxes.

Each method requires a 9inch square baking tin

250g salted butter
170g caster sugar
80g dark brown soft sugar
300g golden syrup
500g jumbo oats

TIP: The darker you cook the flapjacks the crunchier they become, the lighter the more softer and gooier!

Method

- Preheat the oven to 170°C/340°F/gas mark 3½.
- Melt the butter in a thick-bottomed saucepan before adding the golden syrup. Add the sugars and whisk until it forms a thick bubbling caramel. After 2-3 minutes when the sugars have dissolved, pour onto the oats and stir until combined. Do not beat the mix or over work it, as this will make the oats absorb the liquid and the flapjacks will become floury and dry. Spoon into a pre-lined baking tin and flatten. Bake in the preheated oven for 15-20 minutes until golden and bubbling on the outside. Carefully remove from the oven and allow to cool. Cut into squares and store in an air tight container somewhere cool.

Granola Flapjacks

250g salted butter
170g caster sugar
80g dark brown soft sugar
300g golden syrup
500g jumbo oats
25g dried cranberries
25g sultanas
15g pumpkin seeds
15g sunflower seeds
25g hazelnuts
15g flaked almonds

- Use the same method as above, however toast the nuts lightly in the preheated oven for 3 minutes first. Add all the dried fruit, seeds and nuts to the oats.

Millionaire Caramel Shortbread

Biscuit Base
200g room temperature salted butter
100g caster sugar
300g self-raising flour
¼ vanilla pod

8inch square tin

Caramel
200g salted butter
200g dark brown soft sugar
100g condensed milk

Topping
250g dark chocolate

TIP: Don't over mix or handle the biscuit base or it will turn out very chewy and dense.

The Biscuit Base

- Preheat the oven to 180°C/350°F/gas mark 4.
- Cream together the butter, sugar and vanilla seeds, then add the flour and mix slowly until just combined. Spoon into the pre-lined baking tray to cover the base of the tin, and using the palm of your hand gently press into the tin to fill any gaps. Allow to rest for 10 minutes, and then bake for 20-25 minutes until golden brown on top. Remove from the oven and allow to cool.

The Caramel

- Melt the butter in a thick-bottomed saucepan, and then whisk in the sugar and cook for a few minutes until the grains dissolve. Turn the heat down and add the condensed milk whisking all the time. Keep whisking for 3-5 minutes until it starts to thicken and colour, then remove from the heat. Pour onto the cool shortbread and spread evenly. Chill in the fridge for about an hour or until firm.

The Chocolate Topping

- Place the chocolate in a bowl, and suspend over a saucepan of simmering water (a bain-marie) do not allow the bowl to touch the water, until the chocolate has melted. Remove the chilled base from the fridge and pour the chocolate over the top and quickly spread evenly. Return to the fridge. When the chocolate has set, remove and cut into squares.

Fudgy Chocolate Brownies

It's difficult not to love brownies especially when they are as good as these, they are hugely popular amongst my regulars. I don't use cocoa powder in my recipe and I only use very little flour as this keeps them super gooey along with the perfect cooking. These brownies are amazing slightly warmed with proper vanilla custard, fresh raspberries and dark chocolate sauce.

TIP: Remember your brownies will continue to cook when they come out of the oven so every minute counts. Don't overcook!

8inch square tin

6 medium free range eggs
150g caster sugar
150g dark brown soft sugar
200g salted butter
200g dark chocolate
100g self-raising flour
½ tsp baking powder

Method

- Preheat the oven to 170°C/340°F/gas mark 3½.
- Using an electric whisk, mix the eggs and both sugars for about 10 minutes until thick, pale and doubled in volume.
- Meanwhile, place the chocolate and butter in a bowl, and suspend over a saucepan of simmering water (a bain-marie) do not allow the bowl to touch the water, until the chocolate has melted. Remove from the heat and whisk in the sieved flour and baking powder making sure there are no lumps in the mix.
- The eggs should now be ready, so fold half of the mixture into the chocolate, and then the remaining half. Pour into the pre-lined baking tray and put in the preheated oven for approximately 20-30 minutes. When you shake the tin it should only have a slight wobble.
- Remove from the oven and allow to cool. Best to chill in the fridge for 2-3 hours before cutting.

Christmas at
The Dessert Deli

Christmas comes but once a year, and thank goodness as it's one of my busiest times at The Dessert Deli!

It is always a special time of year when everyone seems to have their own favourite sweet or savoury treat. With that in mind, I've included a few of the more traditional festive recipes to help get you in the Christmas spirit.

So top up that mulled wine (unless you're underage of course) and get in the kitchen to prepare some gorgeous homemade gifts or that perfect Christmas cake.

Luxury Christmas Cake

For a Christmas Cake that is deliciously moist, you will need to soak the fruit in port and orange juice in the fridge for a minimum of 2 days, but best left for 3-4. Each day, twice if possible, toss the fruits as the liquid will sink to the bottom of the container, this way all the fruits will be evenly soaked.

Most people 'feed' their cake when cooked, I do the opposite and feed the fruit before it is put in the cake, that way the cake gets really moist as the fruits release their juices.

Soaked Fruits
1kg sultanas
1kg raisins
1kg currants
500g mixed peel
1 x 750ml bottle of port
500ml orange juice

Christmas Cake
200g salted butter
320g dark brown soft sugar
40g black treacle
3 medium free range eggs
200g plain flour
1 pinch of salt
2 tsp ground cinnamon
1 pinch of ground ginger
1.2kg soaked fruits

Extras
1kg marzipan
2kg roll out icing
Apricot jam

Makes 1 x 9inch round cake

Method

- Preheat the oven to 170°C/340°F/gas mark 3½.
- Cream together the butter, treacle and sugar then add the eggs and continue to mix. Sieve the ginger, cinnamon, salt and flour together and add to the mix followed by the soaked fruits. Mix well and scoop into a cake tin, smooth the top and bake in the oven for 30 minutes. Then turn the heat down to 150°C/300°F/gas mark 2 for a further hour to an hour and a half, until the cake is firm to touch and a skewer comes out clean when inserted.
- Allow the cake to cool, then wrap in cling film and allow to firm up over night.
- Place the cake on a cake board. Boil the jam in a pan with a couple of spoonfuls of water just to loosen it slightly. Fill any holes in the cake with small balls of marzipan then brush the cake with the jam. Roll out the marzipan using a light dusting of icing sugar until approximately ½cm thick and then cover the cake with the marzipan making sure there are no holes, either using cake smoothers or your hands to smooth the marzipan onto the cake.
- Repeat the layer of jam onto the marzipan, and repeat the same rolling out process but this time making the icing slightly thicker ¾cm, but you can adjust to your taste. Smooth over the icing and decorate as you wish. Store in an airtight container.

Luxury Mince Pies

This is a seasonal treat loved by the young and old. It's just not Christmas without them! For those of you who aren't so keen on mince pies, try this recipe and I am sure I can change your mind. Made with a fruity, juicy filling and a rich, buttery 'melt in the mouth' pastry, they are divine fresh out of the oven.

Makes approx. 12-16

Mincemeat
400g soaked fruit (page 114 or you can use shop-bought)
200g apple compote (see Apple Pie recipe on page 56 or use shop-bought)
40g dark brown soft sugar
½ tsp ground cinnamon

Pastry
250g room temperature salted butter
225g caster sugar
3 medium free range eggs
500g plain flour

Egg Wash
1 medium free range egg beaten with ½ tsp of milk

Method

- Cream together the butter and sugar until light and slightly fluffy. Slowly add the eggs and continue to mix. Add the sieved flour and mix slowly until all the flour has been combined. Remove from the bowl onto a lightly floured work surface.
- Knead by hand for 1 minute until it forms the consistency of slightly sticky dough. Portion this into 2 blocks, wrap in cling film and place in the fridge to chill for a minimum of 2 hours.
- Once the pastry is chilled, preheat the oven to 170°C/340°F/gas mark 3½ and remove the pastry from the cling film onto a lightly floured surface. Knead this for 1 minute to bring into a ball, then roll using a rolling pin until the pastry is approximately ½cm thick. Keep lightly dusting the surface under the pastry with flour every few rolls to ensure that it doesn't stick.
- To make the mincemeat, chop the apple compote to form a puree, (this helps to bind the mix making it easier to fill the pies) then add the remaining mincemeat ingredients, mix well and set aside. Cut circles in the pastry that are slightly bigger than the cupcake holders of the tin, so that when the pastry is moulded, the top of the pastry reaches the top of the tin. Fill the pastry cases to the top with mincemeat and then cut a circle the same size diameter as the top of the hole and place on top of the mincemeat. Brush with egg wash. Bake in the preheated oven until golden on top. Remove from the oven and allow to cool.

Florentines

These jewelled treats can make a lovely Christmas gift for those friends and family with a sweet tooth.

Makes approx. 24 individual biscuits

TIPS: You can change the fruit used in the Florentines to your preference, however they are traditionally made with flaked almonds as they are thin and work best to help keep the discs flat.

50g salted butter
100g caster sugar
100ml double cream
50g dried cranberries
100g flaked almonds
50g mixed peel
50g sultanas
150g dark chocolate

If you are giving these as a present this is a tip to help improve the presentation. Simply cook for around 7-10 minutes until they just start to brown around the edges. Take them out of the oven and reshape using a cutter. Then put back in the oven for 5-10 minutes to finish the cooking process.

Method

- Preheat the oven to 170°C/340°F/gas mark 3½.
- Place the cranberries, mixed peel, flaked almonds and sultanas in a bowl.
- In a thick-bottomed saucepan melt the butter, then add the sugar followed by the cream and bring to the boil stirring continuously.
- Remove from the heat and pour into the bowl of dried fruits and nuts.
- Stir well then place onto a shallow baking tray and allow to cool for 15 minutes.
- When cooled, spoon 50p sized drops of the mixture onto non-stick parchment/greaseproof paper lined trays approximately 10cm apart.
- Place in the oven for roughly 12-20 minutes or until golden brown.

The Chocolate Base

- Melt half of the chocolate until smooth in a large bowl over a pan of simmering water (a bain-marie) making sure the base of the bowl does not touch the water.
- Remove from the heat, add the remaining chocolate and stir until completely melted. This will cool the chocolate and help temper it so it sets better.
- Once the chocolate is cool but still melted, brush this onto the smooth side of the Florentine and allow to set.

Amaretto Chocolate Truffles

Hand-made truffles are a rich, indulgent way to finish a meal, and guaranteed to impress any guest. Between you and me they're also super easy to make.

Makes approx. 20 individual truffles

TIP: Amaretto can be replaced with another liqueur such as Grand Marnier, Tia Maria or Kahlua or you can leave it out altogether.

CAUTION: Do not over mix the ganache or it will become grainy and may split.

Truffle Ganache
125ml double cream
25ml Amaretto liqueur
200g dark chocolate
15g room temperature salted butter

Truffle Coating
150g dark chocolate
50g cocoa powder

The Ganache

- In a bowl, break the chocolate into small pieces and add the Amaretto.
- In a thick-bottomed saucepan bring the cream to a boil and then pour over the chocolate. Gently mix until all the chocolate has melted.
- Add the softened butter and mix until smooth.
- Pour the ganache into a Tupperware dish ideally 7 x 4 inches with a minimum depth of 2 inches. Cover with cling film and chill in the fridge for a minimum of 4 hours or until firm.
- Portion the mixture into balls using a melon baller, spoon or by hand (if you are using a utensil, dip it in hot water first so the ganache releases easily), and place onto a baking tray covered with a sheet of non-stick parchment/greaseproof paper.
- Place back in the fridge until firm.

The Coating

- Melt the chocolate until smooth in a large bowl over a pan of simmering water (a bain-marie) making sure the base of the bowl does not touch the water.
- Sieve the cocoa powder onto a shallow tray.
- Remove the truffles from the fridge, roll them firstly in the melted chocolate and then place them into the cocoa powder. Shake the tray until they are completely covered. Repeat this process until all the truffles are coated.
- Truffles are best kept in the fridge in an airtight container and served at room temperature.

Cooking with Fruit

TIP: Cut softer fruits bigger, and firmer fruits smaller. This way they can all be cooked at the same time. Remember to remove any stones!

Poaching

- This is ideal if your fruit is under ripe and you need it softer. It is also perfect to use in a cake that cooks quickly so the fruits are soft by the time it is cooked. Poached fruits are lovely served warm with some vanilla ice cream.
- To poach fruits you can use a simple stock syrup (page 128), made up of equal amounts of sugar to water. If you are poaching very hard fruits such as quince increase the water to 1.5 part water to 1 part sugar. As the fruit poaches, the liquid reduces and the syrup will become thicker. You can replace some of the liquid with wine, port, tea or add a few drops of extract into the syrup if you want to infuse with a flavour.
- Bring the syrup to the boil, and then add your fruits. Reduce the heat and cover with a piece of silicone paper and a plate. This keeps the fruit submerged within the liquid. Cook until nearly soft, and then turn off the heat completely and allow to finish cooking in the hot liquid. Allow to cool.

Roasting

3 plums
2 nectarines
2 apples
3 star anise
1 cinnamon stick
1 vanilla pod
200ml port, liqueur or water
50g demerara sugar

- This method creates more crisp, caramelised fruits and it's easier to control than poaching because you can watch through the oven door to see when the fruits start breaking down. Preheat the oven to 180°C/350°F/gas mark 4.
- Place the fruits on a baking tray and drizzle with the port, liqueur or water, sugar, and spices of your choice. I use 3 star anise, 1 cinnamon stick and 1 used vanilla pod. If your fruits are very firm, cover the tray with foil to help soften the fruit, steaming in the juices. Remove the foil after 10 minutes and allow to roast until soft.
- This method is based on using 7-10 fruits, destoned, halved or quartered.

Tuiles, Sauces & Creams

Stock Syrup

A stock syrup is a base recipe which can be kept in the fridge and used when needed. When warm, this is perfect for brushing over cakes to keep them moist and extend their shelf life. It can be flavoured with near enough anything you like such as spices, alcohol or essences.

500ml water
500g caster sugar
½ vanilla pod

- In a thick-bottomed saucepan boil the sugar, water and vanilla seeds for 2-3 minutes. Allow to cool and then store in the fridge. If you do wish to flavour the syrup, replace the vanilla with the addition of your choice.

Tips on Cream

ream is extremely versatile and as outlined in the ingredients page comes in many ways.

Its versatility is best illustrated by how it can change the entire make-up of a dessert depending on how much or how little it is worked.

By whisking/blending we can achieve a variety of consistencies:

Similar to meringues, you can whip cream to form soft or stiff peaks and the same rules apply.
Soft peaks are when the peaks curl over like a breaking wave. Stiff peaks are when the tips of the peaks stand upright when the whisk is removed.
A soft dropping consistency simply means that it should fall off a spoon easily. A thick piping consistency means it is quite dense in texture and will hold its form when piped through a piping bag.

Piping various mixtures, such as cream, can help elevate the level of presentation in your desserts to really wow your guests.

How to pipe cream:
* Spoon the cream into the piping bag until half to three quarters full. Hold the bag loosely just above the nozzle with one hand for support. With your free hand tighten the remaining fabric/plastic at the other end of the bag.
* Gently apply pressure at the back end of the piping bag to release the cream whilst still supporting the bag at the nozzle to help control its direction.

You can also use this method to apply icing to cakes, cupcakes and for piping meringues.

Pastry Cream

500ml milk
100g caster sugar
6 medium free range egg yolks
30g plain flour
1 tbsp cornflour
½ vanilla pod

- Mix the egg yolks and sugar together, and then add the sieved flour and cornflour.
- In a thick-bottomed saucepan bring the milk and vanilla seeds to a boil. Pour the hot milk onto the egg mixture, whisking all the time.
- Return to the pan and bring back to a boil until the custard starts to thicken and coats the back of a spoon.
- Remove from the heat and pass through a sieve into a bowl.
- Place a layer of cling film on top of this mixture to prevent it from forming a skin and chill quickly to prevent further cooking.

Chantilly Cream

500ml double cream
¼ vanilla pod
80g caster sugar

- Pour the cream into a mixing bowl.
- Slice the vanilla pod in half lengthways with a sharp knife and scrape out half of the seeds. Add the seeds and the caster sugar to the cream. Whip the cream until it forms soft peaks.

Crème Légère

200g Pastry cream
50g Chantilly cream

- Beat the pastry cream until soft and then fold in the chantilly cream.
- This is a perfect type to use if you don't like the thickness of pastry cream. I prefer to use this inside profiteroles and éclairs, as with pastry cream this can be flavoured with essences and chocolate.

Lemon Mascarpone Cream

250g mascarpone
20g icing sugar
zest of ¼ lemon

- In a bowl add the mascarpone, icing sugar and lemon zest. Beat all ingredients together until thoroughly combined and then store in the fridge.

Thick Vanilla Custard

This type of custard is ideal for trifles and spreading on scones.

Makes approx. 6-12 portions

500ml double cream
10 medium free range egg yolks
100g caster sugar
¼ vanilla pod

TIP: Have everything ready when making your custard as it needs to be made and chilled quickly to prevent it from scrambling.

- Use the same method as the Proper Vanilla Custard, however cook for 2 minutes when it starts to thicken, then pass through a sieve and chill.

Proper Vanilla Custard

I call this Proper Vanilla Custard as this is how I believe custard should be made and taste. Not like in the supermarkets where if you look at the ingredients, it's thickened with cornflour and then let down with milk. Try for yourself and do a taste test.

Makes approx. 6-12 portions

500ml double cream
5 medium free range egg yolks
80g caster sugar
¼ vanilla pod

- Whisk the yolks and sugar together until combined. Bring the cream and vanilla seeds to the boil and then pour over the yolks and mix.
- Return to the pan on a low heat, stirring continuously until it begins to thicken. Remove from the heat and pass through a sieve into a container and place it in a cold water bath in the sink to chill quickly. Whisk the mix as this will release the heat and cool it quicker. When cold, pour into a container and store in the fridge.

These recipes are constructed to be used as a warm sauce. If you wish to enjoy them cold then add an extra quarter of cream and chill in the fridge.

White Chocolate Sauce

100g white chocolate
100ml double cream

Milk Chocolate Sauce

85g milk chocolate
100ml double cream

Dark Chocolate Sauce

70g dark chocolate
100ml double cream

- Place chocolate in a bowl. Pour the cream in a saucepan and bring to the boil and then pour over the chocolate and whisk until completely melted.

136

Toffee & Pecan

TIP: Pecans, walnuts and hazelnuts go really well with toffee sauce. Roast some nuts and add to the sauce when warm, as this will really bring out their flavour.

This creates a more fudgy tasting toffee sauce using dark brown soft sugar.

300ml double cream
150g dark brown soft sugar
25g salted butter

- Boil the cream and sugar in a thick-bottomed saucepan for 10 minutes. Remove from the heat and whisk in the butter, pass through a sieve. Chill and store in the fridge.

For a lighter, creamier toffee sauce, use the following method:

500ml double cream
250g caster sugar
50g salted butter

- In a thick-bottomed saucepan add the sugar a little at a time until a golden runny caramel is formed, remove from the heat and whisk in the butter. Add a little of the cream and whisk. Be careful as it may bubble away at this point. Once smooth, add the remaining cream. If lumpy, return to a low heat for a minute to warm the sauce slightly, and then pass through a sieve.

Caramel

- This is a dry caramel, which only uses sugar. In a thick-bottomed saucepan on a medium heat gradually add sugar until a runny clear caramel is formed. If you dip a spoon into the caramel, and let it run from a height, it should be crystal clear.
- Caramel decorations should be made and used within the hour, however they do keep well in the freezer for a few hours if you want to make them in advance of a dinner party. You must make sure you put them on silicone paper so they don't stick.
- When making caramel, timing is crucial. Too hot and it won't be pliable, too cold and it will become solid.
- One method is to lay a sheet of silicone paper on the work surface and when the caramel has cooled for a couple of minutes, dip a spoon in and flick a trail all over the paper. This way, when cold, you can break it into shards and use as a garnish.
- To create sugar spirals, rub a metal rod lightly with a little oil. This prevents the caramel from sticking to the rod enabling it to be removed easily. As the caramel cools down it will become quite pliable, and when you can pull the spoon out of the caramel and form a long thin line, it is ready. Hold the rod in one hand and quickly spiral the caramel around it to make a spring.
- To store, fold a piece of silicone paper back and forwards into zig zags, you can then sit the springs into the gaps, and place in the freezer.

Praline

This is a dry caramel using only sugar and nuts.

200g caster sugar
50g nuts of your choice

- In a thick-bottomed pan, gradually heat the sugar until it forms a clear runny caramel, then add the nuts and pour onto a tray lined with silicone paper and allow to cool.
- This can then be crushed with a rolling pin and sprinkled over desserts, or you can blitz it to a fine powder. To make thin caramel discs/squares, sprinkle a layer of powder onto a silicone papered tray, and place back in the oven at 160°C/325°F/gas mark 3 until melted. Then either shape when nearly cool, or allow to cool completely and break into pieces.

Honeycomb

Homemade honeycomb is delicious eaten on its own, covered in chocolate or added to ice cream, cheesecakes and of course my chocolate mousse. When added to the caramel, the reaction with bicarbonate of soda is slightly different every time and reaches very high temperatures.

> *Please be extra careful when making honeycomb!*

250g caster sugar
100ml warm water
2 tsp bicarbonate of soda

- Make sure you have these items ready to hand: 1 sheet of approximately 18 x 30inch non-stick parchment/greaseproof paper, a stepped long palette knife, whisk, heatproof rubber spoon and the measured bicarbonate of soda.

- In a large, thick-bottomed saucepan add the sugar and water and bring to the boil without stirring. Try not to get any sugar on the sides of the pan as this will burn. If any does, use a pastry brush and warm water to clean the sides.

- When it turns a light golden honeycomb colour, remove from the heat.

- Immediately add the bicarbonate of soda, whisk for a few seconds and then quickly pour onto the sheet of non-stick parchment/greaseproof paper. Spread the honeycomb thinly using the palette knife. This ensures the honeycomb cools rapidly and doesn't burn. Leave this until it has cooled completely, before breaking into pieces. Store in an airtight container.

Tuiles

A tuile is a thin, crisp sweet or savoury cookie. Tuile templates can either be bought or made and help produce the perfect shape. In true Blue Peter fashion I use plastic ice cream lids cut to size!

TIP: The smoother the mix the easier it will be to spread. So if you can make it in a food processor or electric mixer this will give you better results. Before baking, you can add various toppings to your tuile mix, such as finely chopped nuts or seeds. If you have a fan oven, weigh the paper down with metal cutlery to stop the fan blowing your tuiles around the oven.

125g room temperature salted butter
125g icing sugar
125g plain flour
2 medium free range egg whites

Method

- Preheat the oven to 160°C/325°F/gas mark 3. Pre-line a baking tray with greaseproof paper.
- Cream together the butter and icing sugar, and then sieve in the flour followed by the egg whites. Mix until a smooth spreadable paste is achieved.
- If you have a template, place on top of the greaseproof paper. If not, then using a stepped palette knife, spread the mix on the paper, until it's 1-2mm thick. Repeat until all the mix has been used.
- Place in the oven for 4-8 minutes until light golden brown. When they are ready, remove from the oven and shape whilst still hot. They can be moulded into cups, around a rolling pin etc. Allow to cool and store in an air tight container.

Brandy Snaps

125g salted butter
125g caster sugar
125g golden syrup
125g plain flour
¼ tsp ground ginger
zest of ½ orange

- Preheat the oven to 180°C/350°F/gas mark 4.
- Melt the butter and golden syrup in a saucepan on a low heat, remove from the heat add the remaining ingredients and combine. Place in a container and allow to cool.
- On a pre-lined baking tray, roll balls of the cooled mixture to about 1 to 1 ½cm round. Space out well on the tray and place in the oven for 10-15 minutes, or until golden.
- Whilst warm these can then be shaped as you wish. You can roll the biscuit around the handle of a wooden spoon to be filled, or make baskets to sit ice cream in. Allow them to cool completely before handling or they may loose their shape.

Cookies

Triple Chocolate

150g salted butter
120g dark brown soft sugar
20g golden syrup
2 medium free range eggs
270g self-raising flour
¼ tsp baking powder
60g white chocolate chunks/drops
60g milk chocolate chunks/drops
60g dark chocolate chunks/drops

* Preheat the oven to 170°C/340°F/gas mark 3½.
* Cream the butter, golden syrup and sugar, before slowly adding the eggs. Now add the sieved flour and baking powder and continue to mix. Then add the chocolate, and mix until combined.
* Divide the mixture into approximately 70g portions, and roll in the palms of your hands, and flatten into 1cm deep discs and place on a pre-lined tray leaving space between each disc as they will spread. Bake in the preheated oven for 10-15 minutes until lightly golden. Allow to cool on the tray. These will be soft and chewy in the middle, but if you prefer a crispier cookie, cook for a further 3-5 minutes.

Cinnamon, Oat & Raisin

150g salted butter
100g light soft brown sugar
35g caster sugar
1½ medium free range eggs
115g self-raising flour
150g jumbo oats
100g raisins
½ tsp ground cinnamon
¼ tsp baking powder

- Preheat the oven to 170°C/340°F/gas mark 3½.
- Cream the butter and sugars, before slowly adding the eggs. The best way to add 1½ eggs, is to add one egg to the mix, beat the remaining egg, and add half. Add the sieved flour, jumbo oats, cinnamon, raisins and baking powder and mix until combined.
- Divide the mixture into approximately 70g portions, and roll in the palms of your hands, and flatten into 1cm deep discs. Place on a pre-lined tray leaving space between each disc as they will spread. Bake in the preheated oven for 10-15 minutes until lightly golden. Allow to cool on the tray. These will be soft and chewy in the middle, but if you prefer a crispier cookie, cook for a further 3-5 minutes.

If you want to play around with different dried fruits and nuts, use the sour cherry recipe and simply replace the cherries and pecans with other varieties.

Sour Cherry & Pecan

150g salted butter
120g dark brown soft sugar
20g golden syrup
2 medium free range eggs
270g self-raising flour
¼ tsp baking powder
¼ vanilla pod
100g pecans
100g sour cherries

- Preheat the oven to 170°C/340°F/gas mark 3½.
- Chop the sour cherries roughly and set aside. Cream the butter, golden syrup, vanilla seeds and sugar, before slowly adding the eggs. Now add the sieved flour and baking powder and continue to mix. Then add the pecans and sour cherries and mix until combined.
- Divide the mixture into approximately 70g portions, and roll in the palms of your hands, and flatten into 1cm deep discs and place on a pre-lined tray leaving space between each disc as they will spread. Bake in the preheated oven for 10-15 minutes until lightly golden. Allow to cool on the tray. These will be soft and chewy in the middle, but if you prefer a crispier cookie, cook for a further 3-5 minutes.

Thank you to all of our wonderful recipe testers

Thank Yous

My Family - You have been my rock and kept me strong, in good times and bad, you have helped get me through each and every day. I love you all very much xx

My Friends – I feel so lucky and proud to have such truly amazing friends. I could not have got where I am today without having such amazing friends as you have all been. Thank you for understanding my crazy busy lifestyle, your help when I have needed it and your company to make me laugh and smile. You are the best friends I could ever wish for xx

My Customers – Thank you to each and every one of my customers who have supported me throughout the years. Of which many of you have become friends over the years and thank you to those of you who participated in the cookbook either in the photo shoot or recipe testing. I am so grateful for your continued loyalty. Supporting me weekly in all weather, come rain or sunshine purchasing desserts and goodies at my market stalls and shops I supply. You are the reason I started The Dessert Deli as I wanted to be a unique dessert brand and make a difference by offering high quality desserts at an affordable price for everyone to enjoy. When I see my customers smiling faces after eating my products, or hear your lovely comments, this always reminds me of why I started the business and what makes the late nights and early mornings all worthwhile. Thank You to Fortnum & Mason and WholeFoods Market for their continued support of The Dessert Deli brand where a selection of my products can be purchased from their prestigious stores. In particular, I would like to thank Fortnum & Mason which I have been lucky enough to have been dealing with for many years now and hope to build the same working relationship with WholeFoods Market in their many stores over the coming years.

My Suppliers – I am very grateful to work with some of the most outstanding suppliers of fantastic first class produce. I truly believe your products taste as good as the ingredients you use to make them. I would like to thank you all for your first class service, professional friendly approach, exceptional quality of products and efficiency of deliveries. Being a small business this has helped me in ways you will never know, so thank you so much and I hope to continue a long working relationship together.

A huge thank you to *Orlando* – Over the years you have grown so much and I am so proud of you and all you have achieved in the kitchen. You work so hard with such passion and pride for your job and always with a smile. I could never have done this without you and I will always be forever grateful for the loyalty, hard work and dedication you have shown to me.

A special thank you to my publishers *Legend Press* (Paperbooks) for making this all possible and for publishing *The Dessert Deli* cookbook. It has been an incredible journey and thank you so much for giving me this amazing opportunity, you have been a great team to work with – Tom, Lauren, Scott, Lucy and Kate xx

A huge thank you to *The Image Pantry*, Mark and Lindsey for their dedication and time on this project producing some fantastic photography within the book, it has been a pleasure working with you both.

It has been a fantastic experience working with both Legend Press and The Image Pantry and would like to thank you both so much, more than words can say for working with me to produce this fantastic book for everyone to now enjoy.

Thank You to:
Mark Hix – Lorraine Pascale – Wendi Peters – Ben Perniha – Yael, Dereck, Solomon Rose & family – Nicky – Adele & Chris – Jacquie & Nick – Katy Truss & Jamie – Craig Ramsden – Mary & Alan – Jason – Louise Keenan – Marion – Richard, Philip, Mikee, Carrie & team at IceBox Logistics – Loretta – Becky & Richard – John Lister, Alan & team at Shipton Mill – Ray Long & team at Meal Maker (UK) Ltd – Johnny & team at The Print Factory SW8 – Bobby, Ruby, Helena & team at Foodspeed Ltd – Tony, Kath, Carl, Trevor & team at HB Ingredients – Harry at Vanilla Mart – Adam & Oliver – Yvette – Chris & Dawn – Jean Claude Lebon at Nobel House UK Ltd – Ewa & RanDiego – Caroline – Kaelie & Steven – Briget – Nathaniel – Ana & Teresa – Harvey, Suzanne, Jane & team at Power Print – Ellie & Kurt – Nina & Dan – Oisin – Kevin Gratton – Phil Usher – Radu & Stefan – Sally & Des – Sarah & Tony – Sarka – Linn – Loretta – Sharon & Julia – Tony – Dave – Vicky & Kelly – Dale – Jass – Mo – Richie Rich & Typhaine xx

Thank you to the following who helped me with props within the book:

On Macarons – www.oncafe.co.uk
WBC – www.wbc.co.uk
Oh! You Pretty Things – www.ohyouprettythings.co.uk
All Good Gifts – www.allgoodgifts.co.uk
Table Manners – www.tablemanners-uk.com

I would also like to thank the wonderful recipe testers whose time and effort ensured that each recipe could be created in the comfort of your own home:

Rachel Findlay	Vanessa Favell	Felicity Spector
Angela Rodger	Clare Anderson	Janet Rogers
Joyce Dooley	Katy Riddle	Nicky Stoney
Jennie Brotherston	Lorraine Cooper	Clare Margary
Cate Kenny	Giulia Mule	Sarah Cobbold
Paul Fox	Maggie Kruger	Jan Hewitt
Laura Henderson	Clare Brierley	Imogen Staveley
Jill Scott	Alison Raven	Bronwyn Wolfe
Ness Gorton	Christina Goodyear	Christopher Troke
Sarah Twinn	Henri Hunter	Corinne Buchan
Laura Pye	Jill Farrimond	Caroline Mills
Jasmine Kershaw		

Index